DRUG DREAMS

DRUG DREAMS

Clinical and Research Implications of Dreams about Drugs in Drug-addicted Patients

Claudio Colace

KARNAC

First published in 2014 by
Karnac Books Ltd
118 Finchley Road, London NW3 5HT

British Library Cataloguing in Publication Data

A C.I.P. for this book is available from the British Library

ISBN 978 1 78049 152 3

Edited, designed and produced by The Studio Publishing Services Ltd
www.publishingservicesuk.co.uk
e-mail: studio@publishingservicesuk.co.uk

Printed in Great Britain

www.karnacbooks.com

CONTENTS

ACKNOWLEDGEMENTS   vii

ABOUT THE AUTHOR   ix

INTRODUCTION   xi

PART I: PHENOMENOLOGY

CHAPTER ONE
Drug dreams: an introduction   3

CHAPTER TWO
Drug dreams: prevalence and general contents   11

CHAPTER THREE
Drug dreams and drug craving   25

CHAPTER FOUR
Drug dreams and abstinence from drug use   39

PART II: CLINICAL AND THERAPEUTIC ASPECTS

CHAPTER FIVE
Clinical and psychological functions of drug dreams   47

CHAPTER SIX
Drug dreams as prognostic indicator   61

PART III: DREAM RESEARCH AND THEORY

CHAPTER SEVEN
Drug dreams and the classic psycho-physiological   71
dream research and theory

CHAPTER EIGHT
Drug dreams and Freud's dream theory   81

CHAPTER NINE
Drug dreams and the neuropsychoanalytic model of dreams   93

CHAPTER TEN
Conclusion and research agenda   103

REFERENCES   111

INDEX   133

ACKNOWLEDGEMENTS

This book completes a series of clinical and experimental observations on dreams about drugs of drug-addicted patients that started in the late 1990s at the Centre for Drug Addictions of Civita Castellana, of AUSL Viterbo (National Health Service, Italy), where I am presently employed as a psychologist and psychotherapist. I wish to thank those colleagues who, through these years, have helped me to complete my studies: Maria Claps, Alessandra Antognoli, Roberta Sperandio, Daniela Sardi, Annalisa Benedetti, Sergio Belsanti, Antonella Antermite, Angelo Galli, Cinza Di Vito, Anna Miscia, Giorgia Giovannini. Special thanks also to the head of Centre for Drug Addiction of Civita Castellana, Angela Lagrutta, who, with her expertise provided me with useful insight concerning the pharmacological treatment of drug addiction and drug craving. My special thanks go to Alessandra Maugeri for her accurate and timely supervision in my efforts to write this book in English. Also, the writing of this book inevitably required time that I could not dedicate to my son Marco and my wife Monnalisa, to whom I extend my thanks for their patience and ongoing encouragement.

ABOUT THE AUTHOR

Claudio Colace is Executive Psychologist at the Operational Unit of Psychology of the National Health Service in Italy—AUSL Viterbo, where he works in the Outpatient Psychology Department and in the Centre for Drug Addictions at Civita Castellana. He obtained an MD in Psychology at the University of Rome "La Sapienza" and a PhD in Psychology at the University of Bologna, Italy. After training in sleep research at the Sleep Laboratory of the University of Rome "La Sapienza", he carried out empirical studies on children's dreams, dream bizarreness, and on dreaming in states of addiction. He was a member of the Italian Society of Sleep Research from 1997 to 2009 and is currently a member of the International Neuropsychoanalysis Society. He is the author of scientific contributions published in *The American Journal on Addictions*; *Neuropsychoanalysis*; *Alcohol and Drug Review*; *Sleep and Hypnosis*; *Sleep*; and *Sleep Research*. He has recently published *Children's Dreams. From Freud's Observations to Modern Dream Research* (Karnac).

For Marco and Monnalisa

Introduction

Drug addiction is defined as a chronic relapsing disease characterised by compulsive drug seeking and use, despite their harmful consequences (American Psychiatric Association, 1994). This disease is a seriously disabling one, and contributes to the deaths of thousands of people every year, in addition to causing major social ills and economic problems for governments due to the extremely high costs of treatment and medical care. One of the biggest problems with drug-addicted patients lies in their frequent relapses (i.e., their returning to use drugs after long periods of abstinence). This phenomenon is due to the typical presence in these patients of drug craving, that is, the impellent desire to use drugs.

It has been pointed out in recent years that one source of access to the vicissitudes of drug craving might be represented by "drug dreams", or those dreams in which drug-addict patients typically use or attempt to use the drugs they are addicted to.

Drug dreams are a well-documented clinical phenomenon in various forms of addiction (e.g., Choi, 1973; Christo & Franey, 1996; Colace, 2004a, 2006, 2010b; Hajek & Belcher, 1991; Persico, 1992; Reid & Simeon, 2001; Yee, Perantie, Dhanani, & Brown, 2004a). Their studies are potentially a very useful resource for the understanding of the clinical and therapeutic aspects of drug dependencies, as well as for their implications for dream research and theory in general.

In the clinical field, for example, some authors have suggested that drug dreams may help patients to remain abstinent (e.g., Choi, 1973; Persico, 1992) or have a "regulatory function" of the drug craving (Fiss, 1980). Drug dreams were also evaluated as a prognostic indicator in the treatment of drug-addict patients (e.g., Choi, 1973; Hajek & Belcher, 1991). Others have suggested that drug dreams might be an alert signal, indicating a heightened drug craving (e.g., Christo & Franey, 1996), or might, indeed, arouse drug craving upon awakening (e.g., Herr, Montoya, & Preston, 1993). In any case, drug dreams were considered a valuable clinical tool throughout the course of the therapy and, generally speaking, a resource for the treatment (Flowers & Zweben, 1996, 1998).

In dream research and theory, since drug dreams often seem to represent the fulfilment (or the attempted fulfilment) of the wish for drugs, they have also been explained according to Freud's classic dream theory (e.g., Choi, 1973; Colace, 2004a; Denzin, 1988; Makaric, 1979). At the same time, the study of drug dreams which refer to a strong motivational state, such as drug craving, has been regarded as a useful research paradigm for the study of the role of motivations in general in the dreaming process (Colace, 2000a, 2001a, 2002, 2004a), a central issue in Solms' recent neuropsychoanalytic theory of dreams (Solms, 1997, 2000). With respect to the latter approach, Johnson (2001) has pointed out that the mesolimbic–mesocortical dopaminergic circuit identified by Solms as essential for the motivational trigger of dreaming is exactly the one that, when exposed repeatedly to addictive drugs, is responsible for drug craving and drug dream onset. Shevrin (1997, 2001) also suggested that drug craving may be seen as a new biological drive in the psychoanalytic sense, which explains the persistence of drug dreams long after the addiction problems have been resolved (e.g., Colace, n.d.a,b; Johnson, 2001).

Drug dreams represent an extraordinary paradigm for the study of dreams in general, and particularly of their psychological functions, where contributions from various disciplines converge: from the clinic therapies for drug dependencies to the neurobiology of drug craving, from the psychoanalytic theory of dreams to dream research, from affective neuroscience to the neuropsychoanalytic model of dreaming. Drug dreams provide an opportunity to view under a magnifying glass the role of wishes in dream processes and contents. This is so because the *craving* for drugs in drug-addict patients represents an abnormal, very strong wish, whose effects on dreaming may be studied and manipulated *in nature* by comparing, for example, the frequency of drug dreams in patients who have stopped using their drugs of abuse or during an abstinent phase (i.e., drug craving frustration) *vs.* those who use drugs regularly, or by studying drug dreams during a phase of sudden recrudescence of drug craving or during its active stimulation due to the presence of drug-related cues.

Finally, since drug dreams are a clear example of non-random and drive-based dream processes and contents, they also offer an opportunity for some new insight in the dream debate, especially in the controversy between those general dream theories that view dreams as non-motivated or random phenomena (e.g., Crick & Mitchison, 1983; Hobson, 1988; Seligman & Yellen, 1987) and those that attribute important emotional adaptive functions to dreaming (e.g., Cartwright, 2010; Freud, 1900a, Hartman, 2011).

*   *   *

The main purpose of this book is to provide a systematic and comprehensive discussion on drug dreams that involves various fields of study and, ideally, to suggest future clinical and research applications. The book draws from personal clinical and research experiences on drug dreams as well as from scientific literature on this topic. My initial interest in studying this type of dreams was quite accidental. During routine psychotherapy sessions, I noticed that heroin-addicted patients often spontaneously reported their dreams about drugs, particularly about using or trying to use them. These dreams were unusually direct and clear in their content, and there was no need for interpretative efforts to understand them. I was immediately impressed because I had direct previous experience of other understandable forms of dreams (clearly related to the dreamers' experience during the awake state), but those had been collected among very young children (Colace, 2010a, 2013; Colace & Tuci, 1996; Colace, Doricchi, Di Loreto, & Violani, 1993). In certain essential aspects, the drug dreams of those patients were similar to the dreams had by children: I am referring especially to brevity and conciseness, direct connection with the dreamer's daytime experience, absence of typical dream bizarreness, and frequent evident presence of the undisguised fulfilment of a wish, that is, in drug addict patients, the desire to seek and use drugs. My interest in these simpler forms of dream was what prompted me to start a more systematic study of drug dreams, mainly among heroin addicts, but also with other drug dependencies (i.e., cocaine, LSD, alcohol). In 1999, I presented some preliminary observations based on four clinical cases at the Congress of the Italian Society of Sleep Research (SIRS), held on the island of Elba (Colace, 1999a; see also Colace, 1999b) followed by other case reports (Colace, 2000b,c, 2001a, 2006, 2009a, 2010b, n.d.a,b) and systematic studies (Colace, 2004a; Colace, Belsanti, & Antermite, n.d.; Colace et al., 2010; Colace et al., n.d). Over the years, my interest shifted from the clinical usefulness of drug dreams to their theoretical and research aspects, that is, to what these dreams might tell in relation to dream research and theories in general, focusing in particular on the implications for Freud's dream theory and the recent neuropsychoanalytic approach to dreaming (Colace, 2000a, 2001a, 2002, 2004a, 2007, 2009b; Colace, Belsanti, & Antermite, n.d.; Colace et al., 2010).

This book is divided into three parts. Part I, "Phenomenology", comprises four chapters. Chapter One is an introduction to drug dreams. It provides a definition of the term and a historical overview of the studies and research topics on these dreams. Chapter Two describes the prevalence of drug dreams, their general contents, and the feelings had while dreaming and upon awakening. Chapter Three, after a digression about the neurobiology of drug craving, deals with the relationship between drug craving and drug dreams, and the effects of certain pharmacological therapies on drug dreams. Chapter Four deals with the relationship between drug dreams and abstinence from drugs.

Part II, "Clinical and therapeutic aspects", consists of two chapters. Chapter Five describes the clinical and therapeutic uses of these dreams, explaining how these dreams may be handled by psychotherapists and physicians in their daily practice. The psychological functions of these dreams are also described. Chapter Six describes their prognostic value.

Part III, "Dream research and theory", is composed of three chapters. Chapter Seven deals with the implications of these dreams for the psychophysiological dream research and theory. Chapter Eight describes the implications of drug dreams for Freudian psychoanalysis, concerning, in particular, the relationship between drug craving and Freud's model of desire and of dream. Chapter Nine deals with the implications of drug dream studies for the neuropsychoanalytic approach to dreaming. Finally, in Chapter Ten, "Conclusion and research agenda", I summarise the main indications deriving from this book and describe what might be the next objectives of studies and researches on drug dreams.

PART I
PHENOMENOLOGY

CHAPTER ONE

Drug dreams: an introduction

Drug dreams: terms and definitions

D rug dreams are a ubiquitous phenomenon among drug-addicted patients. Indeed, these dreams do not appear in people who do not use drugs and/or alcohol and in individuals who, although they use or have occasionally used drugs, are not diagnosed as drug-addicted patients (see Box 1, below) (Colace et al. 2010; Johnson, B., 2011; Johnson, R. A., 2000; Keeley, 2004; Parker & Alford, 2009; Scott, 1968).

The term *drug dreams* appeared in 2001 in a paper by B. Johnson published in the *Journal of the American Psychoanalytic Association*. Johnson used this term in describing those dreams in the contents of which ". . . at least one person was getting high, or there was drug seeking or buying" (Johnson, 2001, p. 86). Other explicit terms appearing in the literature are, for example, "using dreams" (Flowers & Zweben, 1998), "dreams about drinking" (Choi, 1973), "drug-related dreams" (Christo & Franey, 1996; Herr, Montoya, & Preston, 1993), and "relapse dreams" (Washton, 1989) to refer to those dreams on drug/alcohol use or on activities related to drug use. Other authors have used the term "relapse pending dreams", referring to a form of drug dreams that precedes a relapse (e.g., Brown, 1985; Flowers & Zweben, 1998).

Box 1.   *DSM-IV* criteria for the diagnosis of drug dependence

According to DSM-IV (APA, 1994), addiction (or substance dependence) is a term used to denote a condition of drug use (e.g., heroin, alcohol, nicotine) defined by the inability to control it despite the health problems it creates. This condition is manifested by three (or more) of the following criteria, occurring at any time in the same twelve-month period:

1. Tolerance, as defined by either of the following: (a) a need for markedly increased amounts of the substance to achieve intoxication or the desired effect or (b) markedly diminished effect with continued use of the same amount of the substance;

2. Withdrawal, as manifested by either of the following: (a) the characteristic withdrawal syndrome for the substance or (b) the same (or closely related) substance is taken to relieve or avoid withdrawal symptoms;

3. Use in greater amounts or for longer periods than intended;

4. Desire to or unsuccessful efforts to cut down;

5. Considerable time spent in obtaining or using the substance, or recovering from its effects;

6. Important social, work, or recreational activities given up because of substance use;

7. Continued use despite knowledge of the problems caused by or aggravated by substance use;

Although not explicitly listed in the *DSM-IV* criteria, "craving," or the overwhelming desire to use the substance regardless of countervailing forces, is a universally reported symptom of substance dependence.

Sometimes, authors have also introduced more specific terms to describe equally specific kinds of drug dreams. For example, Reid and Simeon (2001), in their analysis of drug dream contents of crack cocaine addicted patients, distinguished the "refusing crack cocaine" dreams from other drug dreams, such as "using crack cocaine", "smelling crack cocaine without seeing it", or "looking for crack cocaine" (without finding it) dreams. Beaman (2002), in alcohol and/or amphetamine addicted patients, described three types of drug dreams: "consuming", "struggling" (i.e., struggling against the craving for alcohol/drug), and "accepting" (i.e., accepting to stay healthy and refrain from using drugs) dreams.

In this book we use the term *drug dreams* to refer to all the dreams where patients use drugs/alcohol, or seek, see, handle, buy drugs/

alcohol (i.e., all the activities related to drug use), or unsuccessfully attempt to use drugs/alcohol, while more specific terms are used for other dreams where the relationship with the drug is of different nature (e.g., refusing the drug).

The historical trend of research on drug dreams

If we look at the story of modern sleep and dream research (Aserinsky & Kleitman, 1953), we may observe that the study of the relations between drugs and dreams started around the 1960s. In those years, some studies analysed the effects of certain psychoactive drugs (e.g., LSD, imipramine) on sleep and dreaming through investigations on the influence of temporary drug administration to healthy volunteer subjects (Arkin & Steiner, 1978; Carroll, Lewis, & Oswald, 1969; Cohen, 1977; Kay, Eisenstein, & Jasinski, 1969; Muzio, Roffwarg, & Kaufman, 1966; Oswald, 1969; Pivik, Zarcone, Dement, & Hollister, 1972; Tart, 1969; Whitman, Pierce, & Maas 1960; Whitman, Pierce, Maas, & Baldridge, 1961).

However, in those years, some authors also began to study the effects of psychoactive substances on the dreams of drug-addicted patients. The dreams of alcoholic patients were the first to be studied (Hall, 1966; Moore, 1962; Scott, 1968) and, as we shall see, alcoholics would remain the most frequently studied subjects, compared to other types of addicted patients, even in subsequent years (Table 1).

The first important study on drug dreams among heroin-addicted patients appeared in the 1970s (Looney, 1972). Looney found a high percentage of drug dreams. He also described the various motives or deterrents which caused the patients to fail to use the drug in their dreams. An early empirical study on the manifest contents of alcoholics' dreams compared to those of non-alcoholics also appeared in the same period (Choi, 1973). Choi investigated the importance of dreams about drinking among alcoholics who were in the process of a therapy. The author concluded that dreaming about drinking is a good prognostic sign in these patients. Choi was also the first author to explain drug dreams by making explicit reference to the Freudian dream theory.

In the 1980s, studies on drug dreams focused mainly on smokers and alcoholics (e.g., Denzin, 1988; Sharpe 1985; Waterhouse, 1984).

Table 1.   The historical trend of studies on drug dreams.*

Alcohol	Heroin	Tobacco	Cocaine	LSD, other drugs
1960s				
Moore, 1962		Baldridge		
Hall, 1966		et al., 1968		
Scott, 1968				
1970s				
Choi (1973)	Looney, 1972			
Alcoholics				
Anonymous,				
1975				
Makaric, 1979				
1980s				
Fiss, 1980		Batson, 1980	Beresford,	Wurmser, 1984,
Reed, 1984		Waterhouse,	et al., 1988;	all drugs
Denzin, 1988		1984; Sharpe,	Washton,	
Meyers, 1988		1985	1989	
Cameron, 1988**				
1990s				
Morrison, 1990;	Christo &	Hajek &	Herr,	Smaldino,
McEwing,1991;	Franey,	Belcher, 1991;	Montoya,	1991, all drugs;
Mooney,	1996	Persico, 1992;	& Preston,	Hernandez,
Eisenberg,	(polydrug	Stewart, 1999	1993;	1992, crack;
& Eisenberg,	patients);		Jerry, 1997;	Kaufman,1994,
1992;	Flowers &		Weinberg,	all drugs
Kibira, 1994;	Zweben,		1996;	
Baireuther,	1996, 1998		Rawson	
1995;	(polydrug		et al., 1993	
Marshall, 1995;	patients);			
Matsumoto et	Colace, 1999b			
al., 1998;				
Parker, 1999				
Schredl, 1999				
2000s				
Peters, 2000;	Colace,		Reid &	Pavlic,
Johnson, R. A.,	2000b,c		Simeon,	Hoffmann, &
2000;	2004a, 2009a		2001; Yee	Rosenberg,
Johnson, B.,	Ivanets &		et al., 2004a;	2009, all
2001, 2003a	Vinnikova, 2001		Colace, 2006	drugs
+ other drugs	narcotics			

(continued)

Table 1.   (*continued*).

Alcohol	Heroin	Tobacco	Cocaine	LSD, other drugs
2000s (cont.)				
Beaman, 2002 + amphetamine;				
Banys, 2002;				
Hoffmann, 2002;				
Araujo et al., 2004;				
Keeley, 2004;				
Ameisen, 2005;				
DeCicco & Higgins, 2009;				
Parker & Alford, 2009;				
Christensen, 2009;				
Jorgensen & Salwen, 2000, alcohol + other drugs				
2010s				
Steinig et al., 2011; Colace et al., n.d.	Colace et al., 2010; Colace, Belsanti, & Antermite, n.d.; Colace, n.d.a		Gillispie, 2010; Colace, n.d.b	Colace, 2010b, mescaline, LSD

* The figure included anecdotal, case report, clinical, and experimental papers.
** Unpublished master's thesis as quoted by Johnson R.A. (2000)

The most important study from this period is that of Fiss (1980), who showed for the first time a clear positive relationship between alcohol craving and dreams about drinking.

After Looney's initial study, other studies on heroin and cocaine addicts appeared in the 1990s (Christo & Franey, 1996; Colace, 1999b; Herr, Montoya, & Preston, 1993). Christo and Franey (1996), studying polydrug users (heroin, alcohol, cocaine, tobacco), found that drug dreams are more frequent in abstinent patients rather than in patients who use drugs regularly. Herr, Montoya, and Preston (1993) concluded that drug dreams are frequent among cocaine-addicted patients and that these are related to drug craving. However, these authors also pointed out that this drug dream phenomenon needed further investigation. In the same period, Flowers and Zweben (1996, 1998) developed a psychoanalytically orientated treatment guide to dream interviewing, with the aim of studying changes in drug dream contents in relation to recovery stages among drug-addicted patients. Also, an extensive study on abstinent tobacco smokers appeared in the 1990s (Hajek & Belcher, 1991), where the authors found two aspects of drug dreams that would later confirm their recurring nature: the dreamer's use of the drug in dreams and the evidence that drug dreams occur mostly during the abstinence from drugs.

It must be said that the publications on drug dreams, at least until the early 2000s, focused mostly on their clinical and therapeutic usefulness, with a certain amount of attention to their descriptive aspects, (see, for example, Reid & Simeon, 2001; Yee, Perantie, Dhanani, & Brown, 2004a) while—save for rare exceptions—the implications of these dreams for general dream research and theory were not considered. On the other hand, studies on drug dreams were often conducted in a purely clinical context and the authors who conducted those studies sought their implications for clinical and therapeutic practice. Rarely were these studies carried out by sleep and dreams researchers. One exception is represented by Fiss's study (1980). Fiss approached the study of drug dreams from the standpoint of the experimental psychology of dreaming and with the purpose of exploring the function of dreams in general. He concluded that drug dreams respond to an intensified drive state (i.e., drug craving), indicating that dreaming, in general, might have a drive regulation function (Fiss, 1980, 1991).

Since the early 2000s, some authors have started to focus on the role that drug dreams may have in general dream research and theory. In fact, due to their prominent motivational origin, drug dreams have been treated with respect to their implications for the study of the role of motivations in dreaming in general (e.g., Colace, 2001a, 2004a, 2009b), for the Freudian dream theory (Colace, 2000a,b, 2001a, 2004a, 2009b), and for the motivational neuropsychoanalytic approach to dreaming (Colace, 2001a, 2004a, 2007; Colace, Belsani, & Antermite, n.d.; Colace et al., 2010; Johnson, B., 2001, 2012; Keeley, 2004; Shevrin, 2001).

Research topics

Although the phenomenon of drug dreams may be observed across all types of drug dependencies, the results obtained by various authors reveal a similar picture of drug dreams among these. From a glance at the literature on drug dreams, different areas of study emerge. Here, I will describe the most important topics in order to provide an overview. Each topic will then be resumed and reviewed in more detail in the subsequent chapters.

One issue addressed by the authors is to determine when drug dreams appear, that is, the *onset of drug dreams and their prevalence in drug-addicted patients and during the therapy* (e.g., Colace, 2004a; Reid & Simeon, 2001). For example, it has been observed that drug dreams appear at the beginning of a therapy, when patients decide to stop using drugs and to remain abstinent, as well as in conditions where the drug is not available (e.g., in a therapeutic community) (Colace, 2004a, 2009a; Colace, Belsanti, & Antermite, n.d.).

Some authors have drawn attention to the effects of *abstinence from drugs on the occurrence of drug dreams*: for example, by comparing groups of abstinent patients *vs.* groups of patients who use drugs regularly (e.g., Colace, 2004a; Hajek & Belcher, 1991). Others have investigated *the relationship between duration of abstinence and frequency and type of drug dreams* (e.g., Christo & Franey, 1996; Reid & Simeon, 2001; Yee, Perantie, Dhanani, & Brown, 2004a).

Some attempts have been made to investigate the influence of the agonist and antagonist medications for a given drug (e.g., methadone as an opioid agonist treatment for heroin) on the frequency of drug dreams (e.g., Colace, 2004a; Colace, Belsanti, & Antermite, n.d.; Hajek & Belcher, 1991).

One of the most studied issues is the *relationship between drug craving and drug dreams.* Drug dream frequency has been correlated to the degree of drug craving as measured by questionnaires and/ or scales, but also by looking at those conditions in which there is an increase of drug craving caused by its frustration or by its active stimulation (e.g., Christensen, 2009; Colace, 2009a; Fiss, 1980; Ziegler, 2005).

Many authors have stressed the *clinical usefulness* of drug dreams and have proposed various *clinical and psychological functions of drug dreams* (e.g., Colace, 2004b; Flowers & Zweben, 1996, 1998; Hajek & Belcher, 1991).

From a strictly clinical and therapeutic view, studies have investigated the possible *prognostic value of drug dreams*. However, a few studies gave conflicting results (i.e., positive *vs.* negative prognosis) (e.g., Mooney, Eisenberg, & Eisenberg, 1992; Persico, 1992). This latter issue also opened the question of the need for a deeper study of *the phenomenology of drug dreams*, targeted to their contents and emotions (during the dream and on awakening), with the aim of classifying the various kinds of drug dreams in relation to prognosis (Brown, 1985; Colace, 2004a,b; Flowers & Zweben, 1996, 1998).

From the point of view of dream research and theory, *the similarities between drug dreams and the dreams that arise under the effects of deprivation of biological drives* such as hunger and thirst (e.g., dreams of food and/or beverages) have been noted (Colace, 2000b, 2004a, 2009b). Indeed, both these kinds of dreams are drive-related dreams mediated by the same neurobiological substrate (i.e., the mesolimbic–mesocortical dopamine pathways). In this respect, *drug dreams* have been considered *as a new methodological opportunity to review the role of wishes* (and of motivations in general) *in dream generation processes and contents* (Colace, 2004a). From this point of view, the phenomenon of drug dreams has been treated as a clinical, theoretical, and experimental *test bench for certain assumptions of the Freudian dream theory*, such as the wish-fulfilment hypothesis, the model of desire, the concept of drive, and the model of psychic apparatus (Colace, 2000a,b; 2001a; 2004a, 2009b; Johnson, 2001; Shevrin, 2001) as well as for the neuropsychoanalytic hypothesis on the dopaminergic motivational triggering of dreams in general (Colace, 2001a; 2004a; Johnson, 2001; Keeley, 2004; Shevrin, 2001; see also Gürpinar & Tokuçoğlu, 2000). Furthermore, recent studies have also focused on an effort to identify—starting from the neuropsychoanalytic approach—the possible *neurobiological correlates of drug dreams* (Colace, 2007, 2009a; Colace, Belsanti & Antermite, n.d.; Colace et al., 2010; Colace et al., n.d.).

CHAPTER TWO

Drug dreams: prevalence and general contents

The prevalence of drug dreams among drug-addict patients

S tudies show that drug dreams are a typical phenomenon among patients addicted to alcohol, heroin, crack cocaine, tobacco, LSD, amphetamine, and other drugs. In my experience, almost all heroin-addicted patients had drug dreams in the course of their past history of addiction or during the treatment.

A sizeable group of systematic studies provides specific data on the prevalence of drug dreams in the drug-addicted population: drug dreams are present on average in about 80% of patients, with the exception of tobacco smokers, who show less frequent drug dreams (33%) (Hajek & Belcher, 1991) (Table 2). A lower frequency of drug/drinking dreams is found only in those studies that consider a very brief period of observation, such as two weeks or less (e.g., Araujo, Oliveira, Piccoloto, & Szupszynski, 2004; Colace et al. 2010; Parker & Alford, 2009).

One of the studies in which the sample is numerically greater is that of Christo and Franey (1996) on polydrug-addict patients (heroin, cocaine, methadone, tranquillisers). These authors, using a drug-related dream questionnaire (occurrence: yes/no), found that out of

Table 2.   Prevalence of drug dreams in drug-addict patients.

Drug	Period of observation	Prevalence	Author
Cocaine+heroin	30 days	91%	Herr, Montoya, & Preston, 1993
Alcohol		90%	Cameron, 1988
Polydrugs	6 weeks	84%	Christo & Franey, 1996
Tobacco	4 weeks	33%	Hajek & Belcher, 1991
Alcohol and/or amphetamine	30 days	97.8%	Beaman, 2002
Crack cocaine	1 month	89.1%	Reid & Simeon, 2001
Cocaine	12 weeks	74%	Yee et al., 2004a
Heroin	Since start of heroin use	66%	Colace, Belsanti, & Antermite, n.d.
Heroin	2 weeks	54%	Colace, 2004a

101 patients, 84% reported having drug-related dreams during the first six weeks of abstinence. These results were also confirmed by a more reliable method of collection of drug dreams: Reid and Simeon (2001) asked crack cocaine addicts (*n* 57) to record their drug dreams daily, upon awakening, for a month, and found that, during the first month of abstinence, drug dreams were reported by 89.1% of patients.

Most studies on drug dream frequency take into consideration the early phase of treatment or recovery of drug-addicted patients—roughly the first two months—and are largely based on the observation of patients who have stopped using drugs/alcohol (i.e., abstinent patients) (Alcoholics Anonymous, 1975; Beaman, 2002; Christo & Franey, 1996; Colace, 2004a; Colace, et al., 2010; Hajek & Belcher, 1991; Kibiria, 1994; Jerry, 1997; Mooney, Eisenberg, & Eisenberg, 1992; Peters, 2000; Reid & Simeon, 2001; Yee, Perantie, Dhanani, & Brown, 2004a). Actually, there are two background conditions in which drug dreams appear very frequently: (a) the *initial period of abstinence from the drug* (i.e., a one or two weeks to two–three months period) and/or (b) *an abrupt and swift transition from daily drug use to a drug-free state* (i.e., abrupt cessation of drug use).

General contents

Drug dreams are often brief, with simple and clear contents that refer directly to daytime experiences and do not require interpretation. From this point of view, drug dreams differ from most dreams of adults (usually long and bizarre). In these dreams, the patient often vividly and intensely experiences the dream scene as if it were a real event (complete loss of reality). Some patients have compared these dreams to dreams of sexual orgasm for the way in which they experienced an intense emotion during their use of drug (i.e., getting high). Several studies agree on the fact that the most frequent content of drug dreams is on drug use (i.e., the patient finds himself using drugs) and on those activities related to drug use (i.e., seeing/seeking drugs, handling or buying drugs/alcohol), (Choi, 1973; Christo & Franey, 1996; Colace, 2000b, 2004a; Colace, Belsanti, & Antermite, n.d.; Colace et al., 2010; Colace et al., n.d.; Herr, Montoya, & Preston; 1993; Looney, 1972; Reid & Simeon, 2001; Yee, Perantie, Dhanani, & Brown, 2004a). Other frequent contents are "unsuccessfully attempting to use drugs" (Table 3).

For example, in a recent study that involved alcoholic patients under detoxification treatment, most of the patients who dreamt of alcohol also consumed alcohol in their dreams (83% were drinking alcohol in their dreams) (Steinig, Foraita, Happe, & Heinze, 2011).

Table 3.   Most frequent themes in drug dreams.

Using drug (or alcohol)
Attempting to use drug
Seeking drug
Preparing drug
Handling drug
Buying drug
Losing drug
Seeing others who use drug
About past problems with taking drugs
Being successful with total abstinence
Being afraid of being caught using drug
Loss of partner as a result of being caught taking drugs/drinking

Herr, Montoya, and Preston (1993) observed that 80% of the drug dreams were about self-administration of the drug, and all dream scenarios included the patient's participation in an activity related to drug use.

Reid and Simeon (2001) observed that during the first month of abstinence, 80.5% of drug-related dreams were about using the drug, and 19.5% about looking for or seeing cocaine.

Yee, Perantie, Dhanani, and Brown (2004a) observed that 75% of the drug dreams reported by cocaine-addicted patients were about using drugs.

Colace (2004a), based on two samples of heroin-addicted patients, found that drug use appeared in about 60% of drug dreams, while other frequent contents implied seeking and attempting to use heroin.

Colace, Belsanti, and Antermite (n.d.), based on a sample of heroin-addicted patients, found the following most common types of drug dreams: dreams on drug use or activities related to drug use (43%) ("using drug" (20%), "seeking drug" (23%), "seeing others using drugs", (11%), "unsuccessfully attempting to use drug" (37%), "fear of being caught", (9%)). Dreams of refusal of drug were not observed.

Hajek and Belcher (1991) found among tobacco-smoking patients that the most frequent forms of drug dreams were about using cigarettes, that is, smoking dreams.

Drug dreams presenting an explicit rejection of the drug have been observed with considerably less frequency in the literature (Beaman, 2002; Colace, 2004a; Colace, Belsanti, & Antermite, n.d.; Reid & Simeon 2001; Yee, Perantie, Dhanani, & Brown, 2004a).

Here, I report some typical examples of drug dreams in different drug dependencies.

Alcohol-addicted patients

I was drinking (no specific setting). I felt apprehension and guilt. (Flowers & Zweben, 1998, p. 195)

We are drinking a champagne toast. Then I begin to go around the room and drink leftover champagne from glasses. Then I am on my fourth glass of red wine and I forget to cover up my drinking. My mother says—'Have you been drinking? Tell the truth' (Johnson, B., 2003a, pp. 148–149)

I was drinking and I was drunk. I was alone and driving the car, and I had an accident. The dream dates back to the time when I stopped drinking. (Case no. 001, personal collection)

I was with some old friends, I was drinking at the bar and got drunk, and then we went to the stadium. The dream was pleasant. (Case no. 002, see Colace et al., 2010)

I was drunk and I felt a feeling of pleasure and at the same time I was bewildered and struggling in the dream, because I knew I should not have done that. When I woke up from the dream, I said thank goodness it was just a dream, it was not something that happened really. (Case no. 003, personal collection)

Heroin-addicted patients

I dreamt I was driving to Rome with a friend of mine to get some heroin. I don't remember the details; however, I remember the scene when I sniffed the drug. The dream was pleasant, and there was no guilt or anxiety associated with its use. While I was sniffing it, I remember an intensely pleasant feeling, as if it were a real-life situation. On waking up in the morning, I didn't feel any particular emotion or any feeling of guilt. (Colace, 2004a, p. 176)

My boyfriend was off seeking heroin and I went with him; I saw syringes. He injected himself, but not me. (Case no. 004, personal collection)

I dreamt that I was injecting myself with heroin. When I woke up I felt a burning desire to use it and then I really used it. (Case no. 005, personal collection)

Excited, I counted the money for heroin and then went looking for it and bought it, but in the end I could not use it. (Case no. 006, dream (a), personal collection)

I was with my friend and I was injecting heroin. (Case no. 007, personal collection)

I was with someone and we were preparing the heroin; a part of it fell on the floor, so I said to my friend, there's too little of it, you use it. I did not use it, and then I woke up. (Case no. 009, dream (a), personal collection)

I was with people in a park and I was injecting heroin. The heroin in the dream was ready for use. I had an intense feeling of pleasure. (Case no. 010, personal collection)

I had an appointment with a friend and I was afraid to take heroin. (Case no. 011, personal collection)

Tobacco-addicted patient

I dreamt I had a cigarette because I'd forgotten I'd given up. Once I finished smoking it, I realized I'd given up. I felt really upset and disappointed, and felt it was bad because I'd forgotten. When I woke up, I felt tremendously relieved that I hadn't smoked really and happy about not smoking. (Hajek & Belcher, 1991, p. 488)

Cocaine-addicted patient

I dreamt I was in the cafeteria teaching other patients here how to chop lines of cocaine and snort them. (Gillispie, 2010, p. 1)

In the dream I had taken a lot of cocaine and I was never tired of making one. I was in a room with friends and my boyfriend. (Colace, 2006, p. 177)

I was with my girlfriend [an addict] and I was doing cocaine. (Case no. 012, dream (a), personal collection)

I was offered cannabis and cocaine. I was uncertain about using it or not, but at the same time I wanted it. (Case no. 013, personal collection)

LSD-addicted patient

I was with friends at a rave party, the people offered various drugs; they gave me LSD and I used it. It was a pleasant dream. (Colace, 2010b, p. 192)

Benzodiazepine

A woman doctor gave me Valium and thought it was okay, even though I was an addict. I was smiling. I really got over. (Johnson, 2001, p. 87)

In some cases, the drug use in the dream is exaggerated compared to reality: the dreamer uses a great amount of drug, or uses it repeatedly. Some patients reported using in their dream a quantity of drugs that they had never used when awake. Furthermore, the exaggerated use of drug may be presented in the dream in the form of a change in the way of drug use: for example, a change from smoking to injecting into the vein (i.e., a way of feeling the effect of the drug faster and more intensely).

> In the dream I used heroin for three days. (Case no. 014, personal collection)

> In the dream, I exclaimed: all this heroin for me, it can't be true! I'll be fine for a week. (Case no. 015, personal collection)

In the drug dreams in which the use of drug fails, the reasons for this are the most disparate and sometimes strange, and also include an abrupt awakening (see Table 4):

> I was preparing myself a heroin shot, which I had not done for many years. While I was preparing it, I felt the usual fear of doing something wrong and spilling the drug, and so it happened. I pulled the plunger backwards too much and the drug started pouring out. Unlike in the past, I was not desperate: I let the drug pour on out, thinking that, after all, it was better that way. (Case no. 016, personal collection)

> I found the money for heroin and then went to buy it but I could not find the pusher. (Case no. 017, personal collection)

> I was running around town with friends looking for a variety of drugs, but when we finally got some, it was taken away by a vague authority of some kind. (Looney, 1972, p. 25)

Table 4.   Reasons for the use of drugs failing in the dream.

The drug is dropped to the ground
The police arrive suddenly
The wind blows the drug away
The pusher cannot be found
The subject suddenly collapses
The subject wakes up
The subject pushes too hard on the syringe and the drug spills out
Parents show up
Some authority representative appears
The subject is stopped by other addicts
The subject receives a phone call

Emotions in drug dreams and upon awakening

The following description of the emotions experienced in the drug dreams and upon awakening is based on the observations made in various studies and on my clinical experience. However, it seems to me that a comprehensive and systematic study on the phenomenology of these dreams has not been attempted so far.

A common type of emotional pattern of drug dreams that has been described in various studies is characterised by the presence of the pleasure in using drugs and the urge to do so, and a feeling of relief upon awakening when the patient realises that no actual use of the substance was made (Choi, 1973; Christo & Franey, 1996; Colace, 2000b, 2004a; Colace, Belsanti, & Antermite, n.d.; Hajek & Belcher, 1991; Reid & Simeon, 2001). For example, some patients look at their arms to spot recent injection marks, then they calm down when they understand what happened and that it was just a dream (Colace, 2000b). Sometimes, the use of drugs in dreams may be followed by feelings of guilt and/or regret (Choi, 1973; Christo & Franey, 1996; Colace, 2000b, 2004a; Colace, Belsanti, & Antermite, n.d.; Denzin, 1998; Hajek & Belcher, 1991; Marshall, 1995; Reid & Simeon, 2001; Scott, 1968; Steinig, Foraita, Happe, & Heinze, 2011; Tracy, 1994). The dreamer's guilty feeling might also appear in the dream content in the form of someone who prohibits and forbids, such as the police, the parents, or other characters. In other cases, drug dreams have been reported where, upon awakening, the patients felt anger and disappointment when realising that they had not really used the drug or that they did not actually have it (Brown, 1985; Colace, 2004a; Colace, Belsanti, & Antermite, n.d.; Flowers & Zweben, 1996, 1998). A third option is also observed, represented by those patients who wake up from drug dreams and feel frustrated because they think that if they have these kinds of dreams, their desire for the drug is so strong that they will never be able to stop using drugs. On this point, Washton (1989), in his study of relapse dreams (dreams of use) about cocaine, suggests that these dreams are disturbing for the patients. This author noted that, when awakening from these dreams, the patients feel disappointed, because these dreams seem to suggest to them that they are not motivated enough to stay drug free. Other types of emotions experienced in the dreams and upon awakening are shown in Tables 5 and 6.

Table 5.   Typical feelings in drug dreams.

Guilt

Panic

Fear

Pleasure/urge of using drugs

Shaking/agitation

Failure feeling

Frustration

Helplessness

Anguish

Regret

Aggressiveness

Anger

Table 6.   Emotional and physical reactions* after awakening from drug dreams.

Relief on realising that the use of drugs was just a dream

Guilt

Anger on realising that drug was not actually used or was not really in the patient's possession

Fear/panic

Anguish

Satisfaction/happiness

Attempt to refuse alcohol/drugs

Vivid thoughts of drugs

Sick feeling

Racing heart

Sweating, shaking

Shortness of breath

Tingling stomach and hands

Restlessness

Ears ringing

* For details on physical reactions, see: Yee, Perantie, Dhanani, & Brown (2004a).

Classifications of drug dreams

Some authors have tried to develop a general classification of drug dreams, starting from certain aspects of these.

One first attempt of drug dream classification based on the patients' emotional response upon awakening was proposed by Brown (1985) for alcoholics. This author found that patients fall into two main categories. A first group of alcoholics *felt frustrated because their dreams were not real*, that is, they had not really consumed the drug. These patients feel compelled to use the drug. The patients in the second group *felt relieved because their dreams were not real*, that is, they had not had a relapse in reality. These patients experienced their dreams as disturbing events because they were determined to not use the substance of abuse and consider actual drug use as repulsive.

Another classification, based on the feelings experienced in dreams and upon awakening, is the one developed by Flowers and Zweben (1996, 1998). These authors draw attention to the major differences between those drug dreams that reaffirm the desire to stay sober, and those that predict an impending relapse.

The so-called "sobriety affirmation dreams" are associated with sense of guilt and worry during the dream and afterwards, and relief upon awakening: "'*I was drinking (no specific setting). I felt apprehension and guilt.*' He felt relieved when he woke up—because he was not drinking in reality" (Flowers & Zweben, 1998, p. 195).

The "relapse-pending dreams" are associated with pleasure in using and disappointment upon awakening at not being high (i.e., disappointment on waking up because "I've not really used heroin"):

> This "very disturbing" dream occurred on an inpatient unit during early recovery . . . *I was with my drug friends. Everybody was getting off. I was shooting up. The needle was in my arm, I could feel it. I felt happy; I was going back to what was safe, familiar, and comfortable.* I awoke before I had any good feeling. I felt disappointed. (Flowers & Zweben, 1998, p. 194)

In Reid and Simeon's study (2001) on crack cocaine abusers, drug dreams were collected together with the relevant emotional responses during the dream and on awakening. On these grounds, the authors found two types of dreamers: the majority of the patients who reported drug-using dreams said they had pleasure and urge feelings while dreaming and no feeling at all on awakening; the majority of the patients who reported refusal dreams felt no emotion during the dream and relief, or no feeling, on awakening.

In my experience, I have tried to classify drug dreams based on their contents. The most interesting aspect that seemingly distinguishes certain dreams from others is whether or not the subject uses the drug successfully in the dream. However, even considering the emotions while dreaming and upon awakening, a wide range of drug dreams appear to fall roughly into two types:

- type A: using the drug;
- type B: unsuccessful attempt to use the drug.

In type A dreams, the patients use the drug and sometimes show feelings of guilt or regret after the use of the drug during the dream and/or upon awakening. Furthermore, in these cases, many subjects showed feelings of relief upon awakening when they realised that they had not really made use of the drug. Actually, the subjects might be strongly determined to remain abstinent or to "stay clean", so they struggle against their drug craving and might experience a strong conflict (see, for example, Sharpe, 1985). In type A drug dreams, we may also include dreams about seeking, buying, seeing, and handling drugs. In these latter dreams, there is also a form of gratification of desire for having drugs available.

Example dreams

> The dream is composed of two scenes. In the first scene, I see a friend who proposes to go and get some heroin. Then I don't remember what happens. In the second scene, I am playing football and the coach approaches me and says something like "I know you use heroin." I can't recall anything else about the dream but I was sure I had used the drug in the dream. I had feelings of guilt and shame. (Case no. 012, dream (b), personal collection)

> I dreamt I was driving to Rome with a friend of mine to get some heroin. I don't remember the details; however, I remember the scene when I sniffed the drug. The dream was pleasant and there was no guilt or anxiety associated with its use. While I was sniffing it, I remember an intensely pleasant feeling as if it was a real life situation.

When I woke up in the morning I didn't feel any particular emotion or any feeling of guilt. (Case no. 018, personal collection)

In "unsuccessful attempt to use the drug" dreams (type B), the attempt to use the drug fails for some—occasionally bizarre—reason. Generally, upon awakening, the subject feels angry, realising that there was no real use of the drug, and might experience a greater urge to use the drug (drug craving increase) (e.g., Colace, 2004a, 2010b). In some cases, the increase in craving lasts throughout the reality of the post-dream day.

Example dreams

I meet a friend and I go get some heroin. I prepare it but when it is ready to take, I wake up. The feelings in this dream were the same as those I have when I am awake, that is, symptoms of abstinence and desire to use heroin. When I woke up I felt intensely disappointed because I had not been able to take the drug. I still wanted heroin when I woke up; I had a strong urge to use it. (Case no. 019, dream (a), personal collection)

I dreamt that the syringe slipped from my hands, I was going to inject, but then I woke up. I felt guilty. Upon awakening I had more desire to use heroin. (Case no. 020, personal collection)

There are, of course, exceptions to the two types of dreams.

The increase in craving and the feeling of frustration due to the failure to use the drug in the dream might also appear in some type A dreams, especially when the dream is not sufficiently satisfying.

In some type B dreams, there might be a feeling of guilt for trying to use substances, followed, in this case, by an emotional reaction upon awakening similar to that of type A dreams, which is a kind of emotional recovery because nothing happened in reality.

Recent data confirm that the anger at not having actually used drugs or, on the contrary, the feeling of relief for not having actually used it, are the two most frequent feelings experienced upon awakening from drug dreams. (Colace, Belsanti, & Antermite, n.d.).

As we shall see later, an adequate phenomenological picture of drug dreams, capable of understanding the differences in terms of content (i.e., use/non use), emotions in dreams, and patients' reactions upon awakening (i.e., absence/presence of a guilty feeling), is fundamental to a correct clinical and prognostic use of these dreams.

CHAPTER THREE

Drug dreams and drug craving

Drug craving: definitions and clinical aspects

*C*raving is defined by the Oxford Website Dictionary as a "powerful desire for something"; other possible synonyms are: *wanting* and *compulsive wishing*.

According to the United Nations International Drug Control Programme (UNDCP, 1992), "drug craving" is "the desire for the previously experienced effects of a psychoactive substance". The main manifestation of drug craving is represented by a sort of tension and internal pressure to seek and consume the substance, and by the presence of obsessive drug-related thoughts. The presence of drug craving is considered one of the distinguishing signs of drug dependence.

Some authors have also described drug craving as a sort of new limbic drive produced by continued drug exposure (Robinson & Berridge, 1993). Indeed, drug-addicted patients experience the urge to obtain and take the drug in order to put an end to a state of inner tension, just as thirst or hunger drives can stimulate to seek food or water (Hutcheson, Everitt, Robbins, & Dickinson, 2001; Koob & Le Moal, 1997).

Drug craving depends on the patient's personal history (e.g., duration of exposure to drugs), his/her personality, and on his/her resilience to stressors—which might also be a case of genetic predisposition (Franklin et al., 2009). Other variables may influence drug craving variations over time, such as the patient's mood, the occurrence of stressful events, the degree of the patient's awareness of the risks related to substance use, and his/her individual capability to cope with drug craving (i.e., the ability to resist or modulate craving). On the other hand, drug craving may be triggered or increased by the availability (or unavailability) of drugs, by the exposure to environmental cues associated with the drug, such as a bar for an alcoholic, or, for a drug addict, the corner of the street where the pusher usually stands.

At least two main components can be described in drug craving. The first is represented by the desiderative–appetitive aspect, or the desire to seek and use the drug in order to re-experience its pleasant effect ("appetitive craving"). The second is represented by the need for the drug in order to avoid painful or adverse withdrawal symptoms ("phobic craving") (see Manna & Ruggiero, 2001; Maremmani, Canoniero, & Pacini, 2002; Petrakis et al., 1999). We shall see how these two components of drug craving act on drug dreams.

Conscious and unconscious aspects of drug craving

While some authors have described drug craving as a conscious desire (e.g., Kassel & Shiffman, 1992; Niaura et al., 1988), others argue that drug craving might be independent of conscious awareness (Berridge & Robinson, 1995; Johnson, B., 2012; Miller & Gold, 1994). The latter authors suggest that it is possible to crave a drug without being aware of it. For example, Childress and colleagues (2008) showed that the response of the limbic reward circuitry could be activated by "unseen" cocaine reward cues (i.e., stimuli with a duration of only thirty-three milliseconds that are not consciously recognised). Furthermore, the increased neuronal activity (in the interconnected ventral pallidum and the amygdala) in response to such "unseen" cues predicted a more positive affective response to visible versions of the same stimuli two days later. This result suggests that the craving for the drug might operate outside awareness and does not necessarily need elaborate cognition, and that environmental drug-related stimuli unconsciously perceived can then lead an unaware subject to risky behaviour and might foster craving in response to drug-related cues (see below; also Ziegler, 2005).

The conscious desire for the drug might, therefore, also be viewed as a qualitative aspect of drug craving that can be more or less present in drug-addicted patients during a given period. The conscious and unconscious aspects of drug craving can be observed, for example, in patients who have been abstinent for years and who consider themselves out of drug dependence. When these patients experience a sudden recrudescence of craving, for whatever reason, this does not occur as a conscious desire right from the beginning, but manifests itself only in drug-related, high-risk behaviours.

Neuroanatomical and neurobiological aspects of addiction and drug craving

Despite the initial specific action mechanism of different drugs, the studies converge in indicating the mesolimbic–mesocortical dopaminergic (ML–MC DA) pathway as the principal area engaged in addiction diseases (Nestler, 2005) (Figure 1).

The most important research paradigms used in investigating the neurobiological and neuroanatomical substrate of drug addiction are the studies on animal models (i.e., self-stimulation, self-administration, and conditioned place preference) and the studies on humans based on recent functional neuroimaging techniques (i.e., positron emission tomography (PET), functional magnetic resonance imaging (fMRI)).

The evidence from both these kinds of studies show that the rewarding effects of drugs are mediated by the activation of the ML–MC DA pathways that arise in the mid-brain ventral tegmental area (VTA) and are projected towards the nucleus accumbens (NAc), the amygdala (and the so-called "extended amygdala"), the hippocampus, the prefrontal cortex, including the orbitofrontal portion (OFC) and the cingulate gyrus (Childress et al., 1999; Daglish & Nutt, 2003; Di Chiara, 1996; Di Chiara & Imperato, 1988; Goldstein & Volkow, 2002; London, Ernst, Grant, Bonson, & Weinstein, 2000; Pulvirenti & Koob, 1990; Sell et al., 1999; Volkow, Fowler, Wang, &

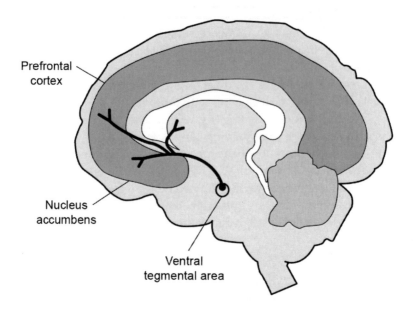

Figure 1.   The mesolimbic–mesocortical dopamine pathway
(adapted from Piomelli, 2001).

Swanson, 2004; Wise & Bozarth, 1987; for a review, see: Koob, 2011;
Koob & Volkow, 2010; Nestler, 2005)

A key site within the limbic system that mediates drug craving is
represented by the globus pallidus and its ventral part, the ventral
pallidum (e.g., June et al., 2003; Robledo & Koob, 1993). The globus
pallidus receives DA fibres from the VTA and the NAc and projects
them, in turn, to the VTA. NAc projections to the ventral pallidum
translate limbic motivation input into motor output. Animal studies
have shown that reward stimuli trigger DA firing in the ventral
globus pallidus (Tindell, Berridge, & Aldridge, 2004). On the other
hand, when ventral pallidum activity is blocked, intravenous drug
self-administration is impaired in laboratory animals (Robledo &
Koob, 1993). Recent functional studies show that the ventral pallidum
is needed for normal reward and is involved in drug seeking and in
motivational wanting (Smith, Tindell, Aldridge, & Berridge, 2009).
Case report studies have shown that a selective bilateral lesion of the
globus pallidus causes the total loss of drug craving of the patient (i.e.,
the craving disappears) without any dysfunction in the executive

functions, or in attention and working memory (Miller et al., 2006; Nigro & Bergesio, 2011), and also causes a reduction in motivation and wanting, apathy, loss of interest, and anhedonia (Brotini, Piani, Dolso, & Gigli, 2005; Vijayaraghavan, Vaidya, Humphreys, Beglinger, & Paradiso, 2008).

An important component of the network that provides the substrate to addiction is constituted by the insular region of the brain that serves subjectively experienced somatic and interoceptive processes such as drug craving (Garavan, 2010). The insula integrates interoceptive states into conscious feeling and plays a crucial role in conscious urges to take drugs (Naqvi & Bechara, 2009). For example, there is evidence of insular activation in the urge for cigarettes. Indeed, smokers with brain damage involving the insula are able to quit smoking easily and will have no persistent craving and no relapse (Naqvi, Rudrauf, Damasio, & Bechara (2007).

Another important aspect of drug addiction involves the mnestic storage of the pleasant effects of drugs. Studies have shown that the memory consolidation of the association between drugs and rewarding experience involves structures such as the amygdala and the hippocampus (Franklin & Druhan, 2000; Meil & See, 1997; Nestler, 2001, 2005).

The DA in the ML–MC system is certainly the neurotransmitter of drug craving. Studies have shown that when drug-addicted patients experience a strong desire for drugs, there is an increase in DA cell firing (Goldstein et al., 2009; Volkow et al., 2006). In particular, the rewarding effects of opiates and other drugs are parallel to the increase of extracellular DA concentrations in the NAc, especially in the "shell" compartment (Di Chiara, 1996; Di Chiara & Imperato, 1988; Pontieri, Tanda, & Di Chiara, 1995; Pulvirenti & Koob, 1990). The DA increase starts during the phase that precedes drug use (i.e., appetitive phase) when drug-conditioned (predicting) stimuli unleash drug craving (Di Chiara, 1995, 1996; Di Chiara et al., 1999).

Thus, the ML–MC dopaminergic system appears to be more involved in the "wanting" than in the "liking" (Berridge & Robinson, 1998; Blackburn, Pfaus, & Phillips, 1987; Brauer, Cramblett, Paxton, & Rose, 2001; Ikemoto & Panksepp, 1996; Leyton, Casey, Delaney, Kolivakis, & Benkelfat, 2005; Leyton et al., 2002; see also Barbano & Cador, 2007).

The importance of the dopaminergic mesolimbic pathway as the neurobiological substrate of drug addiction via the increase of dopamine release in an upregulated manner (i.e., chronic functional changes in the ML–MC DA system) is shared by various neurobiogical theories on drug addiction (see Koob & Volkow, 2010; Wolf, 2002). Particularly interesting for its implications on the relationship between drug craving and dreaming is the "incentive-sensitisation" model of drug addiction (Robinson & Berridge, 1993). According to this model, the repeated exposure to addictive drugs produces persistent changes in the mesolimbic dopamine circuit that normally regulates the attribution of incentive salience to stimuli. These dopaminergic circuits become sensitised to the extent that an abnormal level of incentive salience is attributed to drugs and drug-associated cues. This incentive sensitisation produces an abnormal incentive motivation towards drugs ("abnormal wanting") that persists long after drug use has ceased and appears in the behaviour via unconscious craving or explicit (i.e., conscious) desire for drugs.

Finally, we note that the ML–MC DA system identified by neurobiologists as the substrate for drug dependence was also described in "affective neuroscience" studies. These studies suggest that the ML–MC DA system is the crucial component of the "SEEKING" (Ikemoto & Panksepp, 1999; Panksepp, 1998; Wright, & Panksepp, 2012) or "wanting" systems (Berridge, 2001; Berridge & Robinson, 1998)—that is, the neuronal circuits that are involved in the instigation of goal-seeking behaviours and appetitive interactions with the world (including hunger, sexual desire, or craving for drugs (see Box 2).

The relationship between drug craving and drug dreams

Most authors agree in identifying drug craving as the cause of typical drug dreams in drug-addict patients. From clinical observations, we note that drug dream frequency variations follow the patient's drug craving trend during the treatment. The following types of data support the existence of a close relationship between drug craving and the appearance and/or increased frequency of drug dreams.

Positive correlation between drug craving and drug dreams

Several authors have found a positive relationship between drug craving and the occurrence of drug dreams (Araujo, Oliveira,

Box 2. The SEEKING system

Neurosciences have recently focused on the study of the neuro-anatomic substrate of basic emotions and primary motivations. In this research area, also known as "affective neuroscience" (see Damasio, 1994; LeDoux, 1996; Panksepp, 1998), a series of neuro-anatomical structures which make up the so-called *seeking system* were described (Panksepp, 1998). The main anatomical structure of this system is the mesolimbic–mesocortical dopamine system that arises from the ventral tegmental area (VTA) and projects toward the nucleus accumbens (extended amygdala), ventral pallidum, olfactory tubercle, bed nucleus of stria terminalis, lateral septum, prefrontal cortex, anterior cingulated cortex, basolateral amygdala, hippocampal complex, lateral hypothalamus, lateral mammillary body (Alcaro & Panksepp, 2011; Alcaro, Huber, & Panksepp, 2007). The SEEKING system supports the abilities needed for survival. Its activation is related to curiosity, interest, and expectancy in exploring the outer world in order to obtain what we want (Panksepp, 1998; Wright & Panksepp, 2012). This system is active during "appetitive states", such as hunger, sexual desire, and drug craving. When the *seeking* system becomes inactive or works poorly (e.g., with ageing), a sort of depression develops. When over-stimulated, the seeking system generates forms of behaviour similar to those observed in psychoses, which can be treated with anti-psychotic drugs that reduce dopamine levels. Alcaro, Huber and Panksepp (2007) have described the behavioural functions of the mesolimbic dopaminergic system. In their "affective neuroethological perspective", the activation of the mesolimbic system is seen as the activation of an active organism that, given the effect experienced, generates a tendency to take action (seek) as a true drive. It is, therefore, a sort of disposition. This emotional SEEKING disposition is "an intrisic psycho-behavioural function of the brain, that evolved to cope with all varieties of life-challenging events in unpredictable environments" (Alcaro, Huber, & Panksepp, 2007, p. 15). This disposition has ". . . its own hedonic properties, not the the 'pleasure of satisfaction', but the 'enthusiastic positive excitement', 'interest' 'desire' and 'euphoria' " (p. 16).

Piccoloto, & Szupszynski, 2004; Choi, 1973; Christo & Franey, 1996; Fiss, 1980; Persico, 1992). For example, Fiss (1980) observed that among alcoholics who experienced high craving, 80% reported having drinking dreams, while only 30% of those with low craving had drinking dreams. Choi (1973) noted that drinking dreams among alcoholics appeared after just about three months of abstinence when, clinically speaking, craving usually reaches its highest peak. It should be noted that the measures of conscious craving (i.e., the desire to use the drug) based on self-assessment are not always indicative of the patients' actual drug craving: this could explain the reason why drug craving measures are not always correlated with the frequency of drug dreams (e.g., Steinig, Foraita, Happe, & Heinze, 2011).

Drug dreams during periods of abstinence from drugs of abuse

Drug dreams occur more frequently during states of abstinence from the drugs of abuse, than in the periods in which the substance is used regularly (e.g., Colace, 2004a; see Chapter Four), when we know that there is an increase in drug craving (Di Chiara, 1996; Dimauro, 1999; Koob, 2011; Maremmani, Canoniero, & Zolesi, 1999; Stinus, Le Moal, & Koob, 1990) (see Chapter Four).

Active stimulation of drug craving and sudden appearance of drug dreams

Craving increments obtained by means of active stimulation (in nature or experimentally induced) might favour the appearance of drug dreams. Examples of these situations could be the following: meeting someone who used drugs or whom the patient associates with drug use, seeing a place where the patient had used drugs, elation at having a lot of drugs available, watching a film with scenes of drug use, seeing an object related to drug use, etc. (e.g., see Christensen, 2009; Looney, 1972; Yee, Perantie, Dhanani, & Brown, 2004a; Ziegler, 2005). Ziegler (2005) reported a case in which the reappearance of drinking dreams in a polydrug addict and alcoholic patient who had stayed sober for three years followed his getting hydrocodone (an opioid analgesic) prescribed by his dentist. After the third dose, the patient reported craving for alcohol, and at night he dreamt about his favourite bar and his old drinking buddies. Later, he had a relapse.

Christensen (2009), as an aside in a study on attentional bias toward alcohol-related cues, noted that the presentation of alcohol-related pictures (e.g., glasses of wine or beer; picture presentation, 500 ms) was sometimes followed by the appearance of drug dreams. In particular, Christensen found at least four out of twenty abstinent drinkers who informally reported having "drinking dreams" two to three days after participating in his study.

*Sudden recrudescence of drug craving after a long
drug-free period and reappearance of drug dreams*

The clinical experience has shown that heroin-addicted patients might suffer a drug craving recrudescence and/or relapse after one, two, or more years spent without drugs. In these circumstances, drug craving recrudescence may be anticipated and/or followed by the appearance of drug dreams (e.g., Colace, n.d.,a,b) (see Chapter Five).

*Absence of environmental drug-related cues and
disappearance of drug dreams*

It is interesting to note that, in the absence of environmental drug-conditioned cues that arouse drug craving, drug dreams tend to disappear. For example, when patients who normally report drug dreams change their usual environment, and therefore cease to have their usual drug-conditioned cues, they no longer report any drug dreams.

Examples

> A heroin-addict patient who usually had drug dreams when not using drugs, during a five-month period of abstinence in which he was out and away (in Sweden) from his country (Italy) did not have these dreams. (Case no. 019,dream (b) personal collection)

> A heroin-addict patient under methadone treatment, during the first two months of non-use of the drug, had recurring dreams about heroin. During the third month, he stopped using methadone, too, and the dreams continued. Then, in the following months, he moved to a new environment (went to the USA), and there he had no more of these dreams (no incentive-conditioned stimuli). On the evening of his return to Italy, the dreams returned spontaneously, and the next day he started using heroin again. (Case no. 021, personal collection)

As we shall see later (Chapter Five), drug dreams, in addition to being triggered by drug craving, have themselves an effect on the dreamer's drug craving in the post-sleep period.

Drug craving, pharmacological treatment of drug addiction, and drug dreams

Generally speaking, the goal of pharmacological treatment in drug addiction is to mitigate adverse withdrawal symptoms and attempt to reduce the craving for drugs. While the agonist pharmacological treatment, such as methadone for opiates or gamma-hydroxybutyric acid (GHB) for alcohol, acts more on the "phobic aspect" of craving, that is, the need to avoid withdrawal symptoms (i.e., they act by mimicking the action of drugs), the antagonist treatment, such as naltrexone for opiates, acts by barring the possibility of experiencing the pleasant effect of drugs in an attempt to fight the desire for the drug (i.e., the "appetitive" aspect of craving).

The study of drug dream frequency in patients who are under these different pharmacological treatments which act on different aspects of drug craving might contribute to a better understanding of the same drug craving.

Some studies have shown that drug dreams occur in patients under agonist pharmacological treatment. For example, Hajek and Belcher (1991) observed that smoking-related dreams appear in abstinent tobacco-addicted subjects who receive pharmacological treatment with nicotine chewing-gum (i.e., substitute therapy) to alleviate most of the adverse symptoms, and they concluded that these dreams appear to be generated primarily by cognitive processes of craving rather than directly by falling blood nicotine levels.

The presence of drug dreams was also noticed among heroin-addicted patients under pharmacological treatment with methadone (Colace, 2000b, 2004a, Colace, Belsanti, & Antermite, n.d.; Colace et al., 2010).

In the above-referred patients who take a pharmacological substitute for drugs (agonist), the "phobic" component of craving is supposed to be reduced, compared to subjects who try to stay clean without the aid of agonist pharmacological treatment. However, this does not seem to have prevented the possibility of drug dream occurrence. We interpret these data by assuming that the pharmacological control of phobic-avoidant aspects of craving is not sufficient to remove that portion of the craving that instigates drug dreams. Thus, "phobic craving" is probably not the only factor that can trigger drug dreams. In this regard, the phenomenon of drug dreams that appear suddenly after years of non-use is particularly enlightening (Colace, n.d.a,b). Patients who have been abstinent for years and have come to terms with their past drug dependence might, at some time, report drug dreams that are triggered by drug-conditioned cues which induce a return of drug craving. In these cases, I believe that the reappearance of craving concerns more the "appetitive craving" (i.e., the desire for the pleasant effects of the drug) rather than the "phobic craving", because, as the patient has not been using drugs for a long time, he/she should not fear the withdrawal symptoms.

However, there is evidence that drug dreams occur also in patients who were treated with pharmacological agents that block the possibility of experiencing the pleasant effect of drugs (i.e., "anti-craving" action).

For example, I report here the case of a heroin-addicted patient who was being treated with naltrexone.

> I saw some guys in my party who were using heroin, but I did not, because I was disgusted and I knew I could not use it during naltrexone therapy. When I woke up from this dream I was even more determined not to take heroin. (Case no. 772, personal collection)

Furthermore, drug dreams occur among abstinent heroin-addicted patients who take a high "anti-craving" methadone dosage (70–80 mg/day), and in patients who take buprenorphine, which has a mixed action as a μ-opioid partial agonist/k-opioid partial antagonist (Colace, 2004a, Colace, Belsanti, & Antermite, n.d.; Colace et al., 2010).

A patient on methadone at 80 ml/day reported the following dream:

> I met my pusher near the hospital (the pusher does not live in the hospital area); I was in the car. When I saw him I stopped, he gave me the heroin but then something happened and I could not make one. Upon awakening I was angry because I realised that I had not actually taken heroin, and I was left with great desire. (Case no. 022, personal collection)

A patient on methadone at 70 ml/day reported a decrease in his drug craving, also because when he uses heroin he no longer feels the pleasant effect as before when he was not taking methadone. However, drug craving seems to be still there at an unconscious level, so much so that in the past month since he stopped using heroin, the patient had frequent drug dreams like the one described below:

I was with other people and we went to Rome together to take heroin. Then I used the heroin, but while we were driving back we were stopped by the police. (Case no. 023, personal collection)

A heroin-addicted patient who assumed buprenorphine at 8 mg/day:

I was in some place, I think it was a disco, with a girl. It was a sex dream, friends and other girls were there, everyone was using cocaine. I can't remember if I was using it too, but I think I didn't, in real life I do not snort cocaine, I inject it. (Case no. 024, personal collection)

Choi (1973) noted the presence of drinking dreams also among patients who were taking disulfiram, an aversive treatment for alcohol that causes an unpleasant reaction when alcohol is consumed.

In his study, although the alcoholics who were being treated with disulfiram could remain abstinent for more days compared to those who did not take disulfiram (i.e., better control of drug craving), they continued to report drug dreams. However, in Choi's study, the subjects who had drug dreams and were not taking disulfiram were double the number of those who were taking it. The presence of drinking dreams among abstinent alcoholics who used disulfiram was also noticed in a recent study (Colace et al., n.d.)

Example

An alcoholic, heroin and cocaine addict patient under disulfiram therapy, abstinent from alcohol for ten days, reported the following dream:

I was drinking, I was drunk, I was alone and driving the car, and I had an accident. (Case no. 025, personal collection)

These indications show that even the prevention of the possibility of experiencing the pleasant effect of drugs or the prospect of experiencing unpleasant reactions when alcohol is consumed, with their consequences on the desire for drugs ("appetitive component"), does not remove the possibility of the drug craving instigating drug dreams.

The fact that drug dreams are present in people undergoing therapies that act on different aspects of craving suggests that these pharmacological treatments do not always succeed in effectively reducing drug craving. Its extraordinary strength, far from being tamed, is ready to trigger drug dreams.

On the other hand, Choi's data on the lesser frequency of drinking dreams among subjects who take disulfiram demonstrate that the frequency of drug dreams might represent a reliable indicator of the effectiveness of the medications intended to control a patient's craving. In support of this, I will refer to the following case, which demonstrates the effectiveness of Baclofen (gamma-aminobutyric acid (GABA)) action in reducing alcohol craving and consumption in alcoholics (e.g., Addolorato et al., 2002) as shown and anticipated by the complete disappearance of drinking dreams: Ameisen (2005) reported his experience of an alcoholic patient who, after fifteen days of treatment with Baclofen (gamma-aminobutyric acid) until at 270 mg/day (3.6 mg/kg) on day thirty-seven, did not report alcohol dreams (which usually occurred to him more than once a month) and, after thirty-seven days of treatment, experienced no craving.

CHAPTER FOUR

Drug dreams and abstinence from drug use

Drug dreams as an effect of abstinence

It has been observed that drug dreams occur mostly after cessation of drug use or during early abstinence from drugs, rather than during regular drug use (e.g., Choi, 1973; Colace, 2004a; Fiss, 1980; Hajek & Belcher, 1991; Jerry, 1997; Jones, Krotick, Johnson, & Morrison, 2005; Persico, 1992; Stewart, 1999).

For example, Hajek and Belcher (1991), who studied the drug dream phenomenon in smokers, claim that drug dreams can be viewed as *abstinence effects*. In fact, these authors found that 97% of their sample subjects did not have drug dreams while they were still smoking. In my experience, when patients tell me about drug dreams reported in the past, investigations show that, in most cases, these appeared when they were not using heroin.

Drug dreams are frequent in the initial period of treatment, from the first or second week up to two/three months, in those patients who remain abstinent from drugs. For example, in tobacco smokers, "drug dreams" appeared during the first four weeks of abstinence (Hajek & Belcher, 1991) and in polydrug-addicted patients drug dreams occurred in the first six weeks of abstinence (Christo & Franey, 1996). Jerry (1997) found frequent drug dreams in a cocaine-addicted patient during the early months of treatment and abstinence. In heroin-addicted patients, drug dreams were observed in the first fifteen days of abstinence (Colace, 2004a). In alcoholics, too, "drinking dreams" occur frequently during their initial period of abstinence from alcohol (Alcoholics Anonymous, 1975; Denzin, 1988; Fiss, 1980; Makaric, 1979; Mooney, Eisenberg, & Eisenberg, 1992). For example, Choi (1973) reported that the first three months of abstinence were the ones where "drinking dreams" appeared with more frequency.

On the other hand, a certain minimum period of abstinence seems to be necessary in order to ensure an increase in drug craving which is, in turn, sufficient to trigger drug dreams. For example, a study on tobacco smokers found no drug dreams during 2–5 days of abstinence from smoking (Baldridge, Kramer, Whitman, & Ornstein, 1968). This finding was replicated by Batson (1980), who, after a deprivation from cigarettes that lasted only twenty-four hours, did not detect any increase in drug dreams among the deprived subjects compared to a control group.

Example

A twenty-two-year-old man had been using cocaine every day (daily dose: 1 g) by intravenous injection since he was eighteen when he was admitted, with a diagnosis of cocaine dependence, to psychological treatment. In the first month of treatment, he started to become aware of his problem with cocaine, and he was able to stop using cocaine. During this period, the patient recalled five dreams about cocaine. One of them (the others were similar) was the following:

> I went to buy cocaine in Rome. I bought plenty so that I could make some money out of it [which he never did]. But then I came back and sold just a little, keeping the rest for myself. Then I used it all in a few hours (instead of putting it aside it for the next few days) and so I remained without the drug for a few days and I felt sick.

The dream was pleasant; he felt no guilt after drug use, and no emotions on waking. The patient reported having had dreams like this in the past, but only occasionally and not when he used cocaine regularly, only when he could no longer use 1 g of cocaine every day, but just once a week (Case no. 026, personal collection).

Under abstinent conditions, the patients experience a frustration of their need and a desire for drugs that can lead to an increase in drug craving pressure, which is at the basis of drug dream onset. Indeed, authors have suggested that abstinence produces a motivational state such as a biological drive frustation (e.g., hunger), and increases the motivational impact of the drug-associated cues, multiplying craving intensity (Di Chiara, 1996; Dimauro, 1999; Koob, 2011; Maremmani, Canoniero, and Zolesi, 1999; Stinus, Le Moal, & Koob, 1990). Furthermore, the onset of drug dreams during the early months of abstinence could be explained also by the phenomenon of "drug craving incubation", that is, by a specific increase of craving in response to drug-associated cues (Box 3).

Box 3.   The "incubation of craving"

Studies in rodents, in non-human primates, and in humans have shown that "non-provoked" drug craving and the craving in response to drug-associated cues may have a different trend as the duration of abstinence increases.

Animal studies have shown that cue-induced craving increases during the first several weeks of abstinence and remains high after withdrawal from the drug. This phenomenon is known as "drug craving incubation" and has been observed in association with several drugs (i.e., heroin, cocaine, nicotine, alcohol) (for a review, see Pickens et al., 2011; Shalev, Morales, Hope, Yap, & Shaham, 2001).

For example, Bedi et al. (2011) show that, in cigarette smokers, the craving in response to smoking cues does not only persist but increases with abstinence duration (thirty-five days), even if daily craving (not provoked) and withdrawal symptoms decrease (Bedi et al., 2011).

There are other circumstances in which abstinent patients report drug dreams. These are: conviction, hospitalisation, admission to a therapeutic community, and individual difficulty in obtaining drugs, for example, due to lack of money or due to being detained by the police (Colace, 2009a; Colace, Belsanti, & Antermite, n.d.; Looney, 1972; Yee, Perantie, Dhanani, & Brown, 2004a). Under these circumstances, the deprivation from the drug also might be more drastic (i.e., total impossibility of using drugs), so that an unexpected, consequent greater increase in drug craving may occur. Indeed, under the circumstances above, apart from the effect of early abstinence, there is also the effect of a sort of "abrupt and fast transition" from daily drug use to non-use.

Below are a few examples of patients who have had drug dreams while they were in a therapeutic community and during hospitalisation.

A heroin-addicted patient reported having several dreams of heroin use in the early period since he joined the community. These dreams occurred during the first three months in the community, then, as time went by, they became quite rare. In these dreams, the patient used heroin. The dream pattern was as follows: he was with some friends and went to get drugs and used them. In the dream, he felt intensely vivid and realistic pleasant feelings (those that one feels when using drugs in a state of wakefulness). Upon awakening, the patient said he was disappointed because he could no longer experience the pleasant effect of drug, which had vanished on awakening. He wanted to score and to leave the community. (Case no. 027, personal collection)

A heroin-addicted patient was hospitalised for two weeks after a car accident. During the time spent in hospital he did not use heroin and was only treated with a painkiller, Toradol). He felt a strong desire to try to ask someone to bring him heroin, but then he gave up. During hospitalisation, the patient reported at least seven drug dreams. In all but one of them, he was using heroin. The dream he remembered more clearly was this one (the others were similar): "I was in Rome with friends, we didn't know what to do, then we said—why don't we take heroin? Then we got it and used it. In the dream I used heroin for three days." (Case no. 028, personal collection)

Drug dreams and duration of abstinence from drugs

The frequency of drug dreams decreases gradually after a prolonged period of abstinence. For example, Christo and Franey (1996) showed a decline in the frequency of "drug dreams" in polydrug users after a six-month period of abstinence. Reid and Simeon (2001) showed that after six months of abstinence, drug dreams were reported less frequently than in the first month of abstinence (in crack cocaine addicted patients). Hajek & Belcher (1991), analysing the frequency of drug dreams after three different periods of abstinence (i.e., one month, 1–6 months, and 6–12 months), observed a linear decrease in drug dream frequency. However, their findings did not reach statistical significance.

Some authors also found a change in drug dream contents as the period of abstinence continued. For example, Jerry (1997) showed that, unlike the "using dreams" of the early phase of therapy, the drug dreams reported later on in the treatment process were about having the opportunity to use cocaine, but without using it in the end. Reid and Simeon (2001) observed that after a long period of abstinence (six months, rather than three months) drug dreams were reported less frequently and were more about drug refusal (42% of patients) than drug use (35%). This latter finding was confirmed by another study. Yee, Perantie, Dhanani, and Brown (2004a) observed that drug dream contents in drug-addicted patients switched from drug use (during the first few weeks of study participation) to drug refusal during a thirty-six-week study.

These data suggest that only early abstinence has an effect on drug dream frequency, through the effect it produces on increasing the craving in a patient who is not yet accustomed to stopping using drugs. After a prolonged abstinence, a patient is supposed to be able to accept the non-use of the drug and to experience a less powerful craving.

However, there is also evidence that drug dreams do not disappear completely even after a prolonged drug-free state (Alcoholics Anonymous, 1975; Colace, n.d.,a,b; Denzin, 1988; Mooney, Eisenberg, & Eisenberg, 1992; Flowers & Zweben, 1998; Johonson, B., 2001), and this might be due to the persistence of drug craving over time.

Are drug dreams the result of a "withdrawal syndrome" or physical abstinence?

Some studies allow us to affirm that drug dreams are not, strictly speaking, the result of a "withdrawal syndrome" or physical abstinence (e.g., Colace, 2004a; Hajek & Belcher, 1991). Indeed, several abstinent patients who reported drug dreams were treated with agonist pharmacological medications that *mimic* the effects of the drug of abuse and prevent the onset of adverse withdrawal symptoms by replacing such drugs (see Chapter Three).

From this point of view, drug dreams seem more related to psychological abstinence and to drug craving rather than to a neurochemical deficit *per se*. However, since drug dreams are also present during states of abstinence not treated with agonist medications (Colace, 2004a), we cannot exclude that withdrawal symptoms might have some impact on the onset and on the frequency of these dreams.

Conclusions

In conclusion, drug dreams appear to be connected to the initial phase of abstinence from drugs and/or to a condition in which there is a swift transition from regular use to non-use, which both increase the drug craving pressure. In some less frequent cases, when there is a strong drug craving or its active stimulation, drug dreams may also appear during regular use of drugs. What makes the difference in the likelihood of drug dreams being triggered is the level of intensity of drug craving, which in an abstinent condition is inevitably higher (i.e., increase of the motivational impact of drug-associated cues). In order to be able to trigger drug dreams, the craving must, therefore, reach a certain intensity.

As the abstinence period grows longer (6–12 months) there is a lower frequency of drug dreams, and this is probably due to a decrease in drug craving intensity and/or a greater ability to cope with it on the part of the patient; however, the presence of drug dreams at this stage also might be explained with a sudden return of craving in response to drug-associated cues in the environment.

PART II
CLINICAL AND THERAPEUTIC ASPECTS

CHAPTER FIVE

Clinical and psychological functions of drug dreams

S everal authors have emphasised the clinical and therapeutic usefulness of drug dreams by suggesting that drug dreams can provide information about the patient's drug craving and his/her compliance with the treatment, allowing the clinician to establish appropriate therapeutic strategies (Araujo, Oliveira, Piccoloto, & Szupszynski, 2004; Beresford, Blow, Bower, & Maddahin, 1988; DeCicco & Higgins, 2009; Flowers & Zweben, 1996, 1997; Jerry, 1997; Keeley, 2004). For example, Flowers and Zweben (1996, 1998) suggested that the use of dreams might facilitate the work on addiction diseases at all stages of recovery. DeCicco and Higgins (2009) pointed out that drug dreams provide some helpful insight into the mood of alcohol-dependent patients during recovery. Drug dreams have also been a topic dealt with in the context of group therapy for drug/alcohol-addicted patients (Banys, 2002; Jorgensen & Salwen, 2000; Rawson, Obert, McCann, & Ling, 1993). However, drug dreams also have specific psychological functions with regard to the vicissitudes of personal drug craving and the development of a patient's ability to cope with it. Through drug dream reports, the patients have an opportunity to talk about their desire for drugs and their difficulties in trying to stay clean, which helps them to develop a greater awareness about their disease. This chapter deals with the specific clinical and psychological functions of drug dreams.

Clinical functions

Drug dreams as a "thermometer" of drug craving

Converging clinical and experimental data suggest that drug dreams may provide information on the intensity of a patient's current drug craving, as well as its attenuation and sudden recrudescence (Araujo, Oliveira, Piccoloto, & Szupszynski, 2004; Brown, 1985; Christo & Franey, 1996; Colace, 2000b, 2004a; Fiss, 1980; Larimer, Palmer, & Marlatt, 1999; Sharpe, 1985).

During periods of drug unavailability, the occurrence of drug dreams is a tangible sign of the intensification of drug craving due to the impossibility of its satisfaction. The same applies to the drug dreams that occur during the initial phase of recovery, when the patients struggle against their craving and try to stay clean. On the other hand, when, during the course of treatment, the patients begin to see the benefits of the therapy, showing a greater ability to stay clean and a less powerful craving for drugs, drug dreams tend to decrease in frequency.

As a general rule, drug dreams are an expression of the conscious or subconscious desire to use drugs. However, they might also be an expression of unconscious drug craving pressure. In this latter case, drug dreams may also flag increases in drug craving which the patient is unaware of, and might help patients to gain awareness of this (Araujo, Oliveira, Piccoloto, & Szupszynski, 2004; Colace, n.d. a; Johnson, B., 2003a, 2012; Kibira, 1994; Marshall, 1995; McEwing, 1991; Peters, 2000). Indeed, the level of drug craving perceived is not necessarily the real one. In this perspective, drug dreams might be used to understand the unconscious processes that accompany the recovery from an addiction. For example, Peters (2000) suggested that drinking dreams might help to identify relapse warning signs that would otherwise go undetected.

In the long run, drug dreams might also prove to be a useful tool to verify the effectiveness of the anti-craving action of the pharmacological medication administered to drug-addict patients: for instance, a sudden increase in drug dream frequency might reflect a dangerous increase in drug craving which would call for an adjustment of the anti-craving dosage of the medication.

In conclusion, drug dreams, through their appearance and varying frequency, are a valuable "thermometer" capable of signalling changes in drug craving intensity, including in its unconscious aspects.

Drug dreams as a "window" on drug craving and on the patients' ability to cope with it

The majority of drug dreams are understandable without any need for interpretation and only occasionally they may show certain symbolic aspects. A deeper analysis of the phenomenology of these dreams, including emotions in the dream and upon awakening, might give valuable information on drug craving and on how patients cope with it, as well as on their motivation to stay clean.

The manifest contents of drug dreams shows us how drug craving is satisfied, whether such satisfaction is more or less disguised or straightforward, whether or not it is followed by a feeling of guilt, whether in the dream the attempt to use the drug fails and why, etc. In some drug dreams, apart from drug craving, the patient's motivation to fight his/her use of drugs or to stay clean (i.e., the desire to start a process of change) is also present, albeit with less prominence. This latter instance is evidenced by certain characteristics of drug dreams, such as a feeling of guilt after using the drug, the failure of the attempt to use it, and other indicators. The manifestation in dream contents of the motivation to change, or to stay clean and to fight the drug craving, include:

- presence of guilt;
- failure in the attempt to use substances;
- authorities prohibiting;
- anxiety upon awakening;
- interruption of dream, waking up in anxiety.

Therapists should monitor the contents of the patients' drug dreams and detect the changes in the aspects referred to above.

Flowers and Zweben (1996, 1998) have emphasised the need for, and usefulness of, studying and interpreting the meaning of drug dreams in order to better understand at what stage of the change process the patient is, and to develop the appropriate therapeutic strategies accordingly. According to these authors, the presence of pleasure in "drug use" dreams, and the disappointment upon awakening for not having truly experienced it, is usually a clue that suggests a risk of relapse. These drug dreams indicate that the dreamer is closely tied to drugs and to his/her addiction, which could be a starting point to work on for the therapist. In contrast, guilty feelings in dreams and relief upon awakening might suggest that the patient wants to continue to behave well and stay clean (see also Hajek & Belcher, 1991). On the other hand, the dreams where the patient feels relieved on awakening also suggest that, although the patient wants to remain abstinent, he/she feels internally and externally threatened in his or her sobriety. This should encourage the therapist to explore what is threatening the patient's sobriety and help him/her to manage his/her emotions (Flowers & Zweben, 1998). Flowers and Zweben also suggested that the drug dreams reported in therapy sessions indicate that the patient gets along well with the therapist (e.g., counsellor, psychotherapist, psychologist, psychiatrist, clinician).

According to Gillispie (2010), drinking dreams help alcoholic patients to cope with their desire to drink, and are a signal that these patients are trying to stay abstinent and are ready to be taken into care. In this author's view, it is very important for the therapist to be on the alert to spot any change in these dreams, and become more and more aware of their possible usefulness. For example, the shift from dreams of use to dreams of refusal would indicate the patient's ability to remain sober for longer.

R. A. Johnson (2000) suggested that drinking dreams deserve further research to find out how they might be used to facilitate treatment. Kibira (1994) suggested that the alcoholic dreams of alcoholic women, apart from proving useful in exploring the craving for alcohol and drugs, also allowed the patients to explore their new identity as sober, recovering alcoholics. Araujo, Oliveira, Piccoloto, and Szupszynski (2004) suggested that drug dreams, with their ability to indicate the presence of craving, should help in relapse prevention.

I must say that, over the years, my patients have understood and are well aware of the importance of their drug dreams. They are the first to point out to me their reappearance, their content, and the reactions had upon awakening.

Case example

Mr C, a twenty-eight-year-old man, had used heroin every day (daily dose 1 g) by intravenous injection since he was twenty-five, when he was admitted, with a diagnosis of heroin dependence, to a substitutive drug treatment programme with methadone. In the first period of treatment, the patient reduced the use of heroin drastically (random urine test results were negative). He strongly felt the psychological conflict between his desire to use heroin (drug craving) and, at the same time, his determination to stop using it. Thus, he reported frequent guilty feelings during the state of wakefulness when he used heroin. During this period, the patient recalled, when waking up in the morning, several dreams in which he had used heroin. In these dreams, the patient used heroin in a group situation and enjoyed it physically and psychologically. In some of these dreams, the patient reported having had guilty feelings after using heroin. For example, he was caught using heroin by a family member. Sometimes, the dream was interrupted by an anxious awakening. In general, upon awakening, the patient was glad, happy, and relieved after realising he had not really used heroin. The patient noticed that the frequency of these dreams decreased in proportion to the decrease in heroin craving when awake. Furthermore, later on, dream contents changed: it was no longer he who used heroin; instead, he saw others do so. He reported that it was like watching a film. In the patient's opinion, the longer he kept away from heroin (when awake), the more frequently he had dreams about drug use (see Colace, 2000b). In this case, it is useful to observe the psychological difference between "seeing" and "doing". "Seeing" something forbidden (drug use) implies less guilt, compared to "doing" that something. This change in the patient's dream contents coincided with a reduction in drug craving while awake and an improvement in the progress of the treatment.

Drug dreams as "alert signals" of drug craving recrudescence

The sudden appearance of drug dreams in a patient who has stopped using drugs for a long time and has undergone various changes to improve his/her lifestyle is, in most cases, an undisputed sign of a sudden recrudescence of drug craving, although sometimes only at an unconscious level, and represents a clear warning signal of a possible relapse. In these cases, if the patients are no longer in therapy, they should contact their therapist, while if they are receiving some treatment, the therapist should intensify their analysis sessions. In my experience, in these circumstances, the patients often feel in danger and seek the help of a therapist.

Case examples

A patient addicted to heroin and cocaine, abstinent for eight months, reported the following dream after a few days in which he experienced an increase in cocaine craving:

> I was in a shop. Then I went to a bar, a friend's wife came, eating an ice cream with confectioner's sugar on top (recalling cocaine). Some sugar had fallen on her jacket, so I made a gesture as if to clean it (the sprinkle of "white powder"), but was shouted at by the woman (how dare you put your hands on me!). I left the shop and there were two people using substances, then I found myself alone in front of a McDonald's; I was in my car (the old one I used to have when I took drugs), with the cracked windshield that my ex-girlfriend had broken out of spite. When I woke up I was scared.

The week after this dream, the patient had a relapse: he used cocaine intravenously (see Colace, n.d.,b).

An ex heroin-addicted patient, abstinent for ten years, reported the following dream:

> I met some friends and went to take drugs, I snorted, but while I was doing so I woke up.

The patient did not have any conscious perception of his craving. He had no intentional desire to use heroin. Nevertheless, the dream demonstrates the extraordinary persistence of drug craving. Upon awakening from the dream, the patient's first thought was: how can it be that I still dream of heroin! This dream tells us that the patient might be at risk of relapse. Indeed, later, a thorough clinical check-up showed that this patient had recently suffered a recrudescence of his depression (Colace, n.d.,a).

Psychological functions

Drug dreams as "discharge" of drug craving pressure

Many authors have suggested that drug/drinking dreams can help the dreamer to develop coping strategies against drug craving and stay sober/clean, and have referred to the concept of drug dreams as a "safe way" (e.g., Araujo, Oliveira, Piccoloto, & Szupszynski, 2004; Choi, 1973; Denzin, 1988; Morrison, 1990; Persico, 1991; see also Gillispie, 2010; Schredl, 1999).

Drug dreams seem to allow for a safety compensation, at hallucinatory level, of the continuous urge to use drugs. In this sense, their function is to "discharge" the drug craving pressure.

For example, Choi (1973) observed that alcoholics who reported "drinking dreams" had been tolerating better, and for longer periods, their craving for alcohol compared to alcoholic patients who did not have such dreams. In Choi's words,

> As long as he is able to satisfy his need to drink alcohol through a safe way (in his dreams), he has less internal (preconscious and conscious) anxiety, is able to deal with continuous internal and external stimulation about drinking, and can be abstinent for longer periods of time than those who do not have dreams about drinking. (Choi, 1973, p. 701)

Peters (2000) noted that: "the dream may serve a compensatory function, reflecting the opposite of the dreamer's conscious attitude about drinking" (p. 2) and provides a defence against the desire to drink in order to preserve abstinence.

In line with the hypothesis of the "discharge" function of drug dreams, Kibira (1994) showed that the more patients reported dreams about alcohol and drugs, the less they were depressed.

Finally, Batson (1980) even went beyond the concept of hallucinatory satisfaction in dreams. This author observed that subjects who were deprived of cigarettes for twenty-four hours before going to sleep and had gratifying REM dreams (positive themes of eating, drinking, or cigarette withdrawal scenarios, i.e., oral themes) smoked fewer cigarettes on the following day, compared to those who did not have such dreams. In Batson's words, "dream themes seemed to have bearing on intensity of post-sleep cigarette need" (Batson, 1980, p. 12). Now, these results may be interpreted in the sense that dreams might really end up satisfying the craving for drugs. The results of Batson's study (see also Choi, 1973; Colace, 2004a) are surprisingly in line with the results of an experimental study on (water) drinking dreams. Bokert (1968) observed that subjects deprived of food and liquids who reported gratifying dreams (themes of drinking and/or eating) drank less and rated themselves less thirsty in the period of wakefulness following the dream, compared to thirsty subjects who have not had those dreams (see Chapter Seven for detail). The results of Bokert's study were also supported by Klein (1965), as quoted by Fisher (1970). Is it possible that drug-addicted patients, too, can actually satisfy (even if partially) their cravings in dreams? This question cannot be answered presently; however, the data suggest that many drug dreams might serve as a satisfactory discharge of drug craving. This function of drug dreams is fully consistent with the Freudian theory of dream, as well as with the emotional adaptive theories on dreaming, according to which dreams resolve the emotionally disturbing events of the dreamer's life in various forms (e.g., by containing, contextualising the emotional distress) (e.g., see Breger, 1967; Cartwright, 2010; Fiss, 1980; Hartmann, 2011) (see Chapter Seven).

Case example

> I was with my brother and some friends at home, preparing a meal. I used the stuff (heroin).

The patient used heroin and afterwards he felt guilty. Upon awakening, the desire to use substances appeared diminished. The next day, he did not use drugs (Case no. 030, personal collection).

Drug dreams as "self-aversive" function

For some authors, drug dreams serve as reminders of the adverse consequences of drug use or of drinking, or as reminders of the advantages of staying clean. Thus, they help the patients to prevent relapses (e.g., Choi, 1973; Hajek & Belcher, 1991; Johnson, 2000; Perry, 1997). Hajek and Belcher (1991), in their "aversive conditioning theory", assumed that drug dreams, because of their emotionally negative impact on the dreamer (i.e., panic and/or guilt), might reduce the possibility of repeated drug use. From this point of view,

Hajek and Belcher propose giving more importance to these dreams in therapy (e.g., by promoting their recollection by the patients and focusing the patients' attention on their contents).

Cameron (1988, as quoted by R. Johnson, 2000) found that alcoholics often attribute to drinking dreams the meaning of a reminder that drinking causes problems for them. He suggests that drinking dreams might serve two main functions: they allow the subject to express his/her desire to drink, and, at same time, they help him/her consider his/her current level of sobriety (i.e., a reminder to focus on self protection).

Drug dreams as "incentive" for drug craving

In other cases, drug dreams might even have a function opposite to "discharge", that is, a function of incentivising drug craving.

For example, Christo and Franey (1996) observed that some poly-drug users who had relapses claimed that the presence of drug dreams had contributed to such relapses. According to these authors, it is possible that drug dreams constitute vivid memory recall cues that might provoke drug craving.

This same effect was also found in some tobacco smokers (Persico, 1991).

Mooney, Eisenberg, and Eisenberg (1992) observed that drug dreams could induce drug craving in alcoholics and drug addicts. Yee, Perantie, Dhanani, and Brown (2004a) suggested that drug dreams not necessarily follow a greater craving, but might rather induce drug craving.

Herr, Montoya, and Preston (1993) observed that cocaine-addicted patients, upon awakening from drug dreams, feel the need to use the drug they have dreamt of.

Washton (1989) suggested that, in cocaine addicts, drug dreams produce discomfort upon awakening, and a loss of confidence in their chances of making a change. This aspect, unless properly managed, could lead to actual relapse. In this case, the dream apparently acts as a stressor that might cause an increase in drug craving.

In my experience, I have observed that this incentive effect on drug craving concerns mostly those drug dreams which were not entirely gratifying, or in which the use of drugs failed, or was interrupted by awakening. These drug dreams can trigger drug craving upon awakening and during the following days. By failing to fulfil the drug craving, these dreams eventually turn it on. They act as a sort of appetiser before a meal that is not eaten, leaving one even hungrier. Here, we can distinguish at least two cases: (a) drug craving is increased in post-dream awake state because the dream has failed (fully or partially) in its "discharge" action, or (b) the dream in itself acts as a drug-related appetitive cue for the craving or both factors together.

In any case, it should be taken into account that to wake up with an urge to use the drug is not always associated with a subsequent relapse (Reid & Simeon, 2001). This outcome could depend on how such drug craving increase is treated clinically.

In conclusion, in certain cases, drug dreams might represent an incentive for drug craving that will persist during the state of wakefulness and that, unless handled, might put the patient at risk.

Case examples

A patient reported that, after entering the community, he remembered several dreams about heroin. The patient stayed a few days in the community and then ran away. While in the community, the patient took only 5 ml of methadone per day. The patient said he had not used heroin during the week prior to entering the community. He recalls having had dreams about heroin almost every day while he was in the community. One recurring element of these dreams was the fact that he never succeeded in using heroin in any of those dreams. In every dream, the procedure was the same: meet a friend, go and get heroin, prepare it (spoon, etc.). The feelings in the dreams were the same as during the day, that is, withdrawal symptoms and desire to take heroin. Upon awakening, the patient was left with the desire, and he remembered in particular that, on the last day before leaving the community, he had had one of those dreams that had left a very strong desire for the drug (and he actually used drugs the very evening after leaving the community). (Case no. 019(c), personal collection)

A cocaine-addicted patient reported the following dream:

> I was in Rome where I usually go to take cocaine and I snorted it. In the morning I was happy to discover that in fact I had not really used it. He felt a more intense craving upon awakening. (Case no. 031, personal collection)

Drug dreams are the "guardians of sleep" of drug addicts

Drug craving is a persistent drive during sleep, like hunger, thirst, and other biological drives. Johnson notes that drug dreams are explained by the theory of dreams as the guardians of sleep because, through drug dreams, the patients postpone their motor activity aimed at seeking the drug, satisfy their drug craving, and continue to sleep (Johnson, B., 2003a). Therefore, drug dreams, in common with dreams in general, are supposed to serve the function of guardians of sleep (Freud, 1900a).

Conclusions

A recent study aimed at evaluating what methods are employed in American substance abuse treatment agencies to assess alcohol and drug craving has shown that only four out of 152 respondents claim to use substance-related dreams, and only thirteen respondents use drug-related dreams to recognise that a patient is experiencing craving for alcohol or drugs (Pavlick, Hoffmann, & Rosenberg, 2009).

I believe that the collection of drug dreams should be included regularly in the treatment protocols of drug dependent patients, since we have seen that they provide precious information about the patient's drug craving. Therapists (i.e., counsellors, psychotherapists, psychologists, psychiatrists, clinicians) should develop an attitude of paying attention to the appearance of drug dreams, as well as to their frequency variations. On the other hand, any change in drug dream contents, and in the emotions experienced while dreaming and upon awakening, should also be monitored, with the aim of changing therapeutic actions in response to the patient's current state of drug craving and the strategies adopted to cope with it. The therapist should always encourage patients to pay attention to their dreams, because, through these, they may develop a greater awareness of their craving and of the dangers of relapse, as well as of their potential to drive a change into their lives.

Table 7 shows in synthesis the clinical and psychological functions of drug dreams. Table 8 shows a summary of the possible actions that clinicians may take after being reported their patients' dreams.

Table 7.   Summary of the functions of drug dreams.

Functions		Description
Clinical	*Thermometer*	Changes in drug dreams frequency might signal changes in the intensity of drug craving.
	Window	Dreams allow us to see how the patients interact with drug craving and how it operates. They also allow detection of the patients' determination to stay clean.
	Alert signal	A sudden reappearance of dreams after a prolonged drug-free period indicates that the drug craving is back again.
Psychological	*Self-aversive*	Drug dreams serve as a reminder of the adverse consequences of drug use.
	Discharge	Drug dreams discharge the drug craving pressure (i.e., safe way).
	Incentive	Drug dreams may act as appetitive cue for drug craving.
	Guardian of sleep	Drug dreams ease drug craving and protect the sleep of drug-addicted patients.

Table 8.   Drug dreams and clinical–therapeutic actions.

Drug dreams	Clinical actions
Onset/increased frequency	Assess intensity of drug craving, adjust anti-craving medication, have more frequent sessions in order to help the patient cope with the greater craving.
Prolonged disappearance of drug dreams	This might suggest clinical improvement and reduction in craving. Raise the patient's awareness of such improvement.
Sudden reappearance of drug dreams after prolonged drug-free state	This is almost always a sign of drug craving recrudescence. Monitor craving in the post-dream period. Possibly have more frequent sessions with the patient, in order to help him/her manage the increase in craving before a possible relapse, and also his fear of relapsing.
Drug dreams about unsuccessful attempts to use drug	Verify how the patient relates with his/her craving in the dream. Verify whether the dream might be an expression of the desire to stay clean. Check for greater drug craving upon awakening to prevent relapse.
Dreams about using drugs followed by guilty feelings	Make the patient aware of his/her willingness and ability to fight his/her craving. If the guilty feelings were not present in previous dreams, take note of such change in present dreams.

CHAPTER SIX

Drug dreams as prognostic indicator

A uthors have long attempted to establish whether drug dreams might have some prognostic value in the treatment of drug-addicted patients. However, nowadays, the results emerging from literature are conflicting in this regard (e.g., for a review, see Beaman, 2002; Christo & Franey, 1996; Steinig, Foraita, Happe, & Heinze, 2011) (see Table 9). Even recently, Steinig, Foraita, Happe, and Heinze (2011) have suggested that there is no clear guidance as to the prognostic value of these dreams, and for alcoholics they claim that:

> more studies with larger samples are needed to further investigate the relationship between dreams of alcohol-dependent patients . . . to investigate whether dreaming of alcohol can indeed be seen as a good prognostic factor and prevent possible relapse. (p. 147)

The literature on the prognostic value of drug dreams

Some authors have noticed that drug-addicted patients who have drug dreams are more likely to remain abstinent than those who have no such dreams.

For example, Choi (1973) noted that the alcoholics who are able to satisfy their need to drink alcohol in dreams are able to stay abstinent for longer periods of time compared to alcoholics who do not have drinking dreams; thus, these dreams were considered as a good prognostic sign in the treatment of alcoholics.

Peters (2000) suggested that, in alcoholics, drinking dreams and their supposed "compensatory function" (or "safe way") for the drug craving might prevent a possible relapse.

Makaric (1979) suggested that the dreams of alcoholics in which they fulfil their unquenchable thirst for alcohol might help prevent relapses and suicides.

Kibira (1994) claimed that alcoholic patients who had drinking dreams were abstinent from alcohol for three to nine months, and were less likely to relapse because they were less depressed. Indeed, Kibira found significant negative relationships between being depressed and dreaming about alcohol or drugs, and the incorporation of food, alcohol, and drugs.

According to these results, some direct experiences reported by drinkers testify that they feel that drug dreams express their determination to stay sober (Alcoholics Anonymous, 1975).

In tobacco smokers, Persico (1992) noted that smoking-related dreams were frequent among those patients who were able to be abstinent (drug-free at six months) (45.5% of the drug-free sample) and only one of these dreamers had a relapse. Furthermore, Persico observed that such dreams occurred in the same period when future relapsed patients who did not have drug dreams reported an increased craving.

Hajek and Belcher (1991) observed that tobacco smokers who had "dreams of smoking" were more likely to be abstinent (and, thus, avoid relapses) during the following year than those who did not have similar dreams (i.e., drug dreams as self-aversive stimuli, see Chapter Five).

Reid and Simeon (2001) observed that in crack cocaine addicts a better treatment outcome was associated with having drug dreams at six months follow-up. In particular, the abstinence at six months was associated with having dreams about refusing the drug, or about interacting with it from a distance, rather than with dreams about using the drug. However, the frequency of drug dreams and any feelings had during the dream and upon awakening were not associated with abstinence, and the drug dreams had at the start of therapy were not predictive of treatment outcome (see also Meyers, 1988).

Alternatively to the studies referred to above, other authors have suggested that drug dreams, by signalling the re-emergence of drug craving, might predict an impending relapse and/or suggest a poor prognosis.

For example, Christo and Franey (1996) showed that among poly-drug users, "drug dream" frequency was prospectively related to greater substance use, but this effect was particularly strong with cocaine only (i.e., poor prognosis) (see also Fiss, 1979).

Yee, Perantie, Dhanani, and Brown (2004a) found a negative, U-shaped curve for drug dreams with respect to survival, suggesting that a low frequency of drug dreams was associated with longer survival (i.e., assumed to be good prognosis), whereas no drug dreams at all, or a high drug dream frequency were associated with withdrawal from the study (poor prognosis).

Mooney, Eisenberg, and Eisenberg (1992) suggested that, in alcoholics and drug-addicted patients, drug dreams provoke a craving and are a contributing factor for relapse.

Both lines, that is, those that ascribe to drug dreams a value of positive prognosis and those that ascribe a value of negative prognosis, agree on the fact that drug dreams are signals of the presence of a strong drug craving (Table 9). However, generally, the authors who

Table 9. Drug dreams as a prognostic indicator.

Author	Drug(s)	Prognosis
Choi, 1973)	Alcohol	Good
Alcoholics Anonymous, 1975	Alcohol	Good
Fiss, 1979, 1980	Alcohol	Poor
Meyers (1988)	Cocaine	Good
Hajek & Belcher, 1991	Tobacco	Good
Persico, 1992	Tobacco	Good
Kibira, 1994	Alcohol	Good
Mooney, Eisenberg, & Eisenberg, 1992	Alcohol and drugs	Poor
Christo & Franey, 1996	Cocaine	Poor
Reid & Simeon, 2001	Crack and cocaine	Having drug dreams at six months follow-up = good
Yee, Perantie, Dhanani, & Brown, 2004a	Cocaine	Having few drug dreams = good; no drug dreams at all or high frequency = poor

ascribe a good prognostic value to drug dreams implicitly assume that these have a sort of therapeutic effect, as a safe-way function (e.g., Choi, 1973, Peters, 2000), or as a development of strategies to cope with craving (e.g., Morrison, 1990; Reed, 1984; Schredl, 1999), while the authors who ascribe to them a poor prognostic value implicitly assume that these dreams give evidence of drug craving and they may even increase it (i.e., drug dreams as an induced cue of craving) and predict a relapse (Christo & Franey, 1996). However, both approaches consider the analysis of drug dreams as a helpful clinical tool for insight into drug craving and into the mood of drug-addicted patients, and, hence, for relapse prevention (e.g., DeCicco & Higgins, 2009; Flowers & Zweben, 1998; Parker & Alford, 2009; Rawson, Obert, McCann, & Ling, 1993).

Drug dreams and prognosis: a two-way model

The conflicting results about the prognostic value of drug dreams should be attributed not only to the small number of researches carried out in this area, or to the difficulties in collecting and quanti-fying reliable drug-related dreams (for this debate see: Gerevich, & Meggyes, 2004; Yee, Perantie, Dhanani, & Brown, 2004b), but also to the fact that the studies have often failed to differentiate the contents and the emotions experienced in the dreams and on awakening, with respect to prognosis.

An example of the differentiation of drug dreams in relation to prognosis was that of Reid and Simeon's study (2001) on crack cocaine addicted patients (see above). These authors found that, while all drug dreams are associated with a good prognosis, the strongest effect is associated with "dreams of refusing the drug".

Otherwise, the authors might have considered different types of drug dreams all together, or, on the other hand, only one kind of drug dreams, for prognostic purposes. Not all drug dreams are the same, and not all drug dreams have the same prognostic value. We know that drug dreams can differ in contents, emotions experienced, and emotional reaction upon awakening. Therefore, before proceeding with the evaluation of their prognostic indications, these dreams should be classified in more detail from a phenomenological point of view (Colace, 2001b, 2004a,b). In any case, I believe that drug dreams might give concrete information on the patient's dependence, and on his/her ability to stay clean, only in the short term (about one or two months), and hardly for a longer time.

I have suggested the existence of two types of drug dreams (i.e., type A and type B) (see Chapter Two) among heroin-addicted patients, which might have different consequences for the patients' drug craving (i.e., alleviate or worsen it), with different prognostic values (two-way prognostic model) (Colace, 2001b, 2004a,b). Briefly, when drug dreams are gratifying, by contents and affection (type A, dreams of drug use), they help to mitigate and manage drug craving and may indicate a good prognosis, especially in the short term (i.e., ability to endure abstinence); when drug dreams are not satisfying (type B, dreams of unsuccessful drug use attempts), they might reactivate and/or increase drug craving, which, if not properly managed by therapists, and only in this case, might be the prelude to a relapse.

Obviously, there are variations to this scheme.

The presence of the guilty feelings that sometimes appear after dreaming of using heroin are a further suggestion of the patients' intimate will to change and of the presence of a strong inner conflict between their desire for drugs and their desire to stop using drugs and stay clean.

The dreams in which drug use fails (type B dreams) might sometimes be the expression of a resistance to drug use. This, in itself, could be indicative of a future successful treatment (good prognosis). Indeed, in some of these dreams, there is a feeling of guilt for trying to use the drug. On this point, Looney (1972) already affirmed that dreams of failed use might represent a fulfilment of the desire to stop using drugs and remain clean. However, for these dreams, the most relevant clinical question remains the treatment of increased craving in post-dream reality.

At times, the same increase in drug craving in post-dream reality might also occur in type A dreams, if they turn out not to be fully satisfying.

To sum up, the basic assumption of the proposed two-way prognostic model is that drug dreams try to have, via the hallucinatory fulfilment of the desire for drugs, a "discharge" effect on drug craving pressure. According to our theory, the greater the gratification of drug craving in dreams (i.e., emotional discharge), the more the prognosis will be a favourable one. In this regard, Fiss (1980) found that the drinking dreams of patients with low craving contained themes of drug craving gratification (i.e., "drinking and feeling happy"), whereas the drinking dreams of patients with high craving contained defensive and conflictual themes (e.g., "loss of a love object as a result of being caught drinking" (Fiss, 1980, p. 152)).

This proposed model can "explain" the apparently conflicting results of some studies, with drug dreams viewed sometimes as signs of a good prognosis, and sometimes of a poor prognosis.

This model is based on heroin addicts, and yet integrates well with previous models based on the dreams of alcoholics and those of poly-drug abusers.

The existing models were developed by Brown (1985) and Flowers and Zweben (1998), starting from the classification of drug dreams based on the analysis of emotions in dream contents and on awakening (see Chapter Five).

In Brown's model (1985), the emotions appearing in the drug dreams and on awakening, rather than their contents, may give prognostic indications. Those patients who have drug dreams where a sense of frustration prevails because the dreams are not real are described as those who will later relapse and who tend to use drugs. I have ventured the hypothesis that this sense of frustration on awakening is more present in type B dreams (Colace, 2004a). On the contrary, those patients who have drug dreams where they are soothed by the fact that it is only a dream and not reality are those who are more willing to follow the treatment and are encouraged not to use substances.

Flowers and Zweben (1998) stated that the so-called "relapse-pending dreams" are associated with the pleasure in using drugs and the disappointment felt upon awakening for not really being high (i.e., poor prognosis). On the contrary, "sobriety affirmation dreams" are associated with guilt, sense of worry in the dream and afterwards, and relief upon awakening (i.e., good prognosis).

In Figure 2, I have tried to integrate the above-described models of drug dream prognostic value as a rough guide for future studies on this topic.

The continuous lines refer to the "two-way model" (Colace, 2004a), the dotted lines to the model of Flowers and Zweben (1998), and the broken lines to the model of Brown (1985).

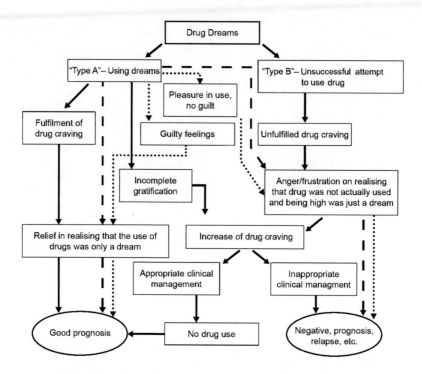

Figure 2.   An integrated prognostic model of drug dreams in drug addiction.

PART III
DREAM RESEARCH AND THEORY

CHAPTER SEVEN

Drug dreams and the classic psycho-physiological dream research and theory

I t is widely known that for a long time the study of the role of motivations in dreaming processes has received, with rare exceptions,
very little attention in the classic psycho-physiological dream
research and theory (see, on this topic, Antrobus, 2001; Colace, 2010a;
Smith et al., 2004). For example, in 1977, McCarley and Hobson
suggested that REM sleep and dreaming are due to an automatic and
cyclical brainstem neural mechanism and that, therefore, the underlying causal mechanism of dreaming is "motivationally neutral"
(p. 1219). Later, in the 1980s, the psychological cognitive approach put
great emphasis on the description of dream generation processes, by
assuming that the issues of dream meaning and dream motivation
could be temporarily omitted (e.g., Foulkes, 1985). This trend has
reversed only recently, due to the results of functional neuroimaging
and neuropsychological studies of dreaming that have shown how the
forebrain areas, including the frontal and limbic structures involved
in the individual's basic emotions and motivations, play a key role in
dreams (Braun et al., 1997; Maquet et al., 1996; Nofzinger, Mintun,
Wiseman, Kupfer, & Moore, 1997; Solms, 1997, 2000). However, many
years before these results, several authors found the clear effects
of biological drive frustration on dreams (i.e., "the biological drive

frustration paradigm"), by emphasising the role of motivations in instigating the dream (i.e., Baldridge, 1966 and Baldridge, Whitman, Kramer, Ornstein, & Lansky, 1965; Bokert, 1968; for review, see Arkin & Antrobus, 1991; Colace, 2009b), but, unfortunately, these studies received little attention from the scientific community. This chapter highlights the ways in which drug dreams can offer a good methodological and conceptual dream framework for the study of the motivational determinants of dreaming and in support of the studies on the effects of biological drive frustration on dreams.

Drug dreams as a new conceptual framework and research paradigm for the study of the motivational bases of dreaming

There is little doubt that drug craving plays a key role in triggering and determining drug dreams; indeed, we have seen that these dreams are ubiquitous in drug-addicted patients who have drug cravings and are not present at all in people who use drugs sporadically and in healthy people (see Chapter One). We might now assume that this motivational state *causes* the dreams related to it (i.e., the drug craving instigates dreams according to a cause–effect relationship), or that it *increases the incidence and the frequency* of these dreams (i.e., correlational relationship). In both cases, it can be affirmed that drug dreams are a clear example of how a motivational state is actively involved in the generation processes of such dreams. However, there is another fact that should be taken into account: patients do not have drug dreams all the time, but only or mostly when they are in an abstinent state and experience a greater drug craving, or when their drug craving is revived or stimulated by drug-related stimuli (i.e., during acute craving episodes). This indicates that drug craving is not present in drug dreams as a mere emotional residue of the daytime experience (if it were so, drug dreams would also appear in drug-addicted patients who use drugs regularly and satisfy their craving every day), but, rather, that drug craving acts as a strong motivational instigator of these dreams.

On the other hand, in drug dreams, the craving for drug appears in a specific way, that is, mostly in the form of its attempted gratification, rather than in other non-specific ways (i.e., generic presence of drugs). These dreams have a clear meaning: that of satisfying the desire for drugs, sometimes successfully and sometimes not. From this point of view, drug dreams seem to be finalised and motivated psychological acts, more than random processes.

We have seen how drug dreams relate to aspects of post-dream motivated behaviour, especially with respect to drug seeking behaviour and drug use. For example, the patients who report gratifying drug dreams succeed in remaining abstinent for longer periods than those who do not have drug dreams or, vice versa, sometimes certain drug dreams may increase drug craving in post-dream reality: both cases show that drug dreams are intimately related to the motivational state that generated them, in the sense that drug dreams are affected by the motivational state (i.e., drug craving) and have themselves an influence on it.

In conclusion, from the point of view of the general dream research, drug dreams represent another piece of evidence (see below) that motivational states should not be neglected in the study of dreaming processes. They offer a clear example of non-random and motivation-based dreaming processes and contents.

From a methodological point of view, drug dreams offer certain advantages in the investigation of the relationship between motivational states and dreaming processes: in the first place, because drug craving is a quantitatively abnormal motivation that may be observed "in nature" and is easily identifiable in dream contents. In the second place, knowing the neurobiological substrate of drug craving—which is the same as other basic biological drives—we may develop hypotheses about the neurobiological events that co-occur during drug dreams (see Chapter Nine).

The study of the effects of biological drive frustration on dreams and drug dreams

In the classic psycho-physiological dream research, one of the study areas that clearly proved the importance of motivational determinants in dreaming is that of the studies on the effects of biological drive frustration on dream contents (i.e., the "biological drive frustration paradigm"). These studies cover various research areas and deal with the effects of the frustration of different type of vital needs (see Arkin & Antrobus, 1991; Colace, 2009b; Fisher & Greenberg, 1977; Kline, 1971; Ramsey, 1953). A recent review (Colace, 2009b) has identified studies that, despite coming from different research areas, share the fact that they allow us to observe the effects of the deprivation of individual vital needs in the dream content directly, without any interpretative work. I will report some examples below.

Studies on the effect on dream contents of the deprivation of food and/or liquids

In Bokert's classic study (1968), a group of eighteen subjects were deprived of food and water, and, before going to sleep, they received a salty meal, while the subjects in the control group were not deprived of food and water and ate a normally salted meal. Another group of subjects, in addition to the above conditions, before waking from REM sleep, received a recorded verbal stimulus saying "a glass of iced water". Bokert (1968) found that drinking-related contents were more frequent in the group of subjects who had been "deprived" and received the voice stimulus before awakening. These contents were, in any case, more frequent (compared to the control group) also in the deprived subjects who did not receive the verbal stimulation. Bokert (1968) also found that the subjects report gratifyng dreams (themes of drinking and/or eating), when they woke up, drank less and were less hungry than those who did not have dreams of satisfaction.

Studies on the effect of imprisonment and social isolation on dreams

Wood (1962) found that subjects who have been in social isolation for a day had dreams, during the subsequent period of REM sleep, that referred, in a more evident manner compared to a control group, to social activities and interactions, such as, for example, "conversation groups or meetings" and, more generally, about "socialising". Andersen (1975) observed that the war prisoners in Vietnam quite frequently dreamt about their desire to "go home" (back-home dreams) and about the typical gestures of an ordinary daily routine.

Studies on the effect of sterility on dreams

Berger (1980) studied the dreams of women who had learnt that their husbands could not procreate. He observed that about 60% of them reported dreams in which "they were happily pregnant".

Studies on the dreams of paraplegic disabled individuals

Newton (1970) observed that the dreams of individuals affected by a recent paralysis (paraplegics and quadriplegics) contained a greater quantity of movement visuals compared to those of normal subjects. Money (1960) observed that the dreams of a group of twenty-one paraplegics suffering from total paralysis of the genito-pelvic area contained images of sexual orgasm. These results were confirmed in a subsequent study by Ryan (1961).

Studies on the dreams of individuals who have suffered amputation of a limb

Shukla, Sahu, Tripathi and Gupta (1982) studied the dreams of seventy-two subjects who had recently undergone the amputation of a limb. In the dreams of thirty-one of these (43%), their limbs appeared intact. A similar result was found by Mulder, Hochstenbach, Dijkstra, and Geertzen (2007), who noted that, in most dreams of people who had had an amputation, the subjects continued to visualise their limbs. These indications were confirmed in a review that considered the dreams of people born without a limb (Brugger, 2008).

Cases known by the general public

A significant experience was that of the famous actor, Christopher Reeve, who became popular in the role of Superman. As a consequence of a bad riding accident, the actor suffered the breakage of his spinal column. He revealed that, during the first two months when he was bedridden, he dreamt of being healthy, riding horses, playing with his children, and making love with his wife (news reported in AA.VV., 1995). The following is another case that lends itself well to proving the appearance of similar dreams: Alexis, a patient known for being the first to receive a transplant of both hands, reported having had the following dream a little before surgery: "I dreamt I was buttoning my shirt" (news reported in AA. VV., 2000, p. 12).

Now, I believe that the case of drug dreams supports and strengthens the biological drive frustration paradigm (see Figure 3). Indeed, drug dreams as biological drive-related dreams and impellent need-related dreams often represent an attempt to gratify the frustrated drives.

BIOLOGICAL DRIVE FRUSTRATION PARADIGM

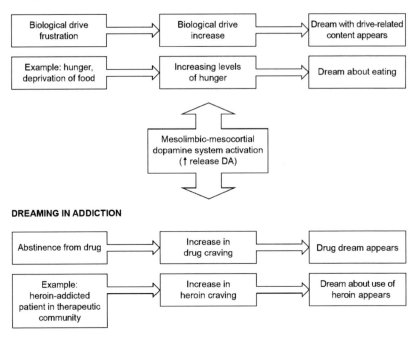

DREAMING IN ADDICTION

Figure 3. Motivational states and dreaming processes: convergences between drug dreams and biological drive frustration paradigms.

In psychological terms, as in the case of drug dreams, the frustration of a biological drive or an impellent need in the pre-sleep period is correlated with the onset of dreams that represent in a clear form their gratification (or attempted gratification).

Drug dreams and biological drive-related dreams are based on drives that share the same neurobiological substrate. The mesolimbic–mesocortical DA system that mediates drug craving is usually involved in the effect of reinforcing biological drives, such as food and sex, and in those activities that keep us alive, and in other social and cognitive rewards (Aragona et al., 2006; Blackburn, Pfaus, & Phillips, 1992; Fibiger & Phillips, 1987; Kelley & Berridge, 2002; Koob & Le Moal, 2006; Lieberman & Eisenberger, 2009; Melis & Argiolas, 1995; Tobler, Fiorillo, & Schultz, 2005; Wise, 1989;); there is an increase of DA in the NAc (nucleus accumbens) during the appetitive (i.e., anticipatory) state in biologically motivated behaviours (eating, drinking, copulating), as well as in drug craving (Bassareo & Di Chiara, 1999; Blackburn, Pfaus, & Phillips, 1992; Damsma, Pfaus, Wenkstern, Phillips, & Fibiger, 1992; Di Chiara, 1995, 1996; Romo & Schultz, 1990).

In addition, addictive drugs are considered as "reinforcers" in the same way as food and water (see Falk, Dews, & Schuster, 1983; Nader & van der Kooy, 1994; Young & Herling, 1986).

In both the above paradigms, we note the exceptional nature of the motivation behind the dream. This "exceptionality" concerned, in the case of drug dreams, the pathologically abnormal nature of drug craving and, in the case of biological drive-related dreams, the extraordinary power of biological drives or of other impellent needs. Both these situations arise as a privileged starting point to study the influence of motivations on the dream, and should be implemented in the future.

Finally, we note that the data emerging from both these kinds of studies can provide a clear example of the motivational triggering of dreams, which is consistent with the frontal and limbic neuronal activation in dreaming found in recent neuroimaging and neuropsychological studies (Braun et al., 1997; Maquet et al., 1996; Nofzinger, Mintun, Wiseman, Kupfer, & Moore, 1997; Solms, 1997, 2000).

Drug dreams and current theories about dreaming

We have observed that drug dreams are a clear expression of motivational vicissitudes. These dreams, like other types of dreams (e.g., biological drive-related dreams and wish-fulfilment young children's dreams, see Colace, 2009b, 2010a, 2013), lead to the reconsideration of those dream theories according to which the mechanism of dream activation is "motivationally neutral" (McCarley & Hobson, 1977, p. 1219), or dreams are merely the by-product of REM sleep state (i.e., a forebrain synthesis of PGO—ponto–geniculo–occipital random and chaotic stimulation) (Hobson, 1988, Hobson, Pace-Schott, & Stickgold, 2000). Also, in the recent updates to Hobson's position, dreams are considered the mere subjective epiphenomenon of REM sleep, carrying out their function of maintaining the optimal functioning of consciousness (i.e., "REM sleep–dream protoconsciousness hypothesis" (Hobson, 2009; Hobson & Friston, 2012). On the other hand, drug dreams are equally inconsistent with the "reverse learning" theory (Crick & Mitchison, 1983) and with Seligman and Yellen's neurocognitive model (1987), both inspired by the above-mentioned neurobiological approach. As they stress the role of PGO random activation, they both claim that dreams are inherently meaningless. In Seligman and Yellen's neurocognitive model, although the authors suggest that certain current concerns (including wishes and biological motivations) may direct the emotional setting of dream plots, they have no role in dream instigation. All the models referred to above may be defined as non-motivational approaches to dreaming and they cannot predict the onset, the incidence, and/or increase in frequency of drugs dreams as a result of drug craving frustration.

The phenomenon of drug dreams, in particular their function of discharging craving pressure, is somehow compatible with the emotional adaptive theory of dreaming in its different versions, as well as with recent "emotional–motivational" hypotheses about the function of sleep and dreams (see Table 10; Box 4). For example, the assumption that dreams may resolve emotionally disturbing events in the dreamer's life in various forms (e.g., by containing or contextualising

Table 10.   The most important emotional–adaptive theories of dreaming.

Authors	Functions of dreams
Freud, 1900a, 1916–1917	Dream serves to discharge instinctual energies. Dream preserves sleep by treating the stimuli that disturb it.
Breger, 1967; Breger, Hunter, & Lane, 1971; Fiss, 1980; Cartwright, 1996, 2010	Dream resolves emotionally disturbing events.
Revonsuo, 2000	Dream serves a biological and adaptive function by simulating threatening events and improves the dreamer's ability to cope with threats during state of wakefulness.
Hartmann, 2011	Dream reduces the intensity of emotional distress or calms emotional storms.
Kramer, 2007	Dream serves as mood regulator.
Nielsen & Levin, 2007; Levin & Nielsen, 2007	Dream serves to facilitate fear memory extinction.
Fosshage (1997)	Dream serves as regulator and restorer of psychological organisation and affectivity.

Box 4:   Emotions and motivation in recent sleep and dream research

The emotional dissipation theory of sleep and dream

Recent MRI (fMRI) studies show that sleep has an important role in emotional brain processing (Yoo, Gujar, Hu, Jolesz, & Walker, 2007; Van der Helm & Walker, 2009; Van der Helm et al., 2011). These studies show how a night of sleep contributes to "dissipating" the emotional charge via amygdala activity in response to recent daytime emotional experiences, and, hence, how it ". . . may 'reset' " the correct affective brain reactivity to next-day emotional challenges by maintaining the functional integrity of this (medial prefrontal cortex) mPFC–amygdala circuit and thus govern appropriate behavioural repertoires . . ." (Van der Helm & Walker, 2009, pp. 10–11) and reduce next-day subjective emotionality.

The Reward Activation Model for sleep and dream

The Reward Activation Model (RAM) for sleep and dreaming has recently proposed that dreaming is the result of the amplification of the activation of the mesocortical–mesolimbic DA system due to privileged reactivation during sleep of the ". . . memories with high emotional and motivational value for the individual" (Perogamvros & Schwartz, 2012, p. 1942). From this point of view, the authors suggest that dreaming may have a role in learning and memory as well as in emotion regulation processes.

---

the emotional distress) (see Breger, 1967; Cartwright, 2010; Fiss, 1980; Hartmann, 2011) matches with the observation that drug dreams have helped drug-addicted patients to handle drug craving stimulation and remain abstinent. However, we note that the adaptive theories of dreaming are aimed more at explaining how dreams incorporate emotions, or, in other words, the emotional function of dreams, rather than at explaining the underlying processes of their motivational instigation.

The hypothesis of drug dreams as a "safe way" for drug craving (i.e., discharge of *craving pressure*) is also consistent with the "affective re-establishment" function of children's dreams (Colace, 2013) according to which wish-fulfilment dreams in children (most of the dreams of young children) resolve an affective state and provide an affective reestablishment through the fulfilment of a wish (see Box 5).

Conclusions

The classic psychophysiological dream research has neglected the study of the role of motivational states in the triggering of dreams.

Box 5.   The "affective re-establishment" function of children's dreams

Recent studies (Colace, 2010a, 2013) suggest that children's wish-fulfilment dreams appear to be built on the memories of recent, intense affective experiences of the dreamer's life with an accurate spatial–temporal connotation. In particular, the elements (or components) of these dreams appear to be connected to memories of emotional experiences that—due to being too strong or too recent—have not been psychologically processed and elaborated. Thus, from the point of view of memory-related sources of dreaming, one can assume that the criterion by which the memory system selects the elements that make part of these dreams is motivational, emotional, temporal, and relates to emotional intensity.

The majority of the wishes fulfilled in these dreams arose and were active during the dreamer's recent daytime life, where they were associated with an intense emotional state that was not fully processed psychologically and, therefore, resulted in some kind of disturbance. The dream puts on stage the hallucinatory fulfilment of these wishes and resolves the associated affective state. Through the elaboration of daytime affective experience, the dream allows the child to obtain emotional restoration and to continue sleeping undisturbed. In other words, wish-fulfilment dreams resolve an affective state and provide affective re-establishment.

This "affective re-establishment" function hypothesis based on children's dreams is consistent with the emotional adaptive theories of dreaming based on adults' dreams (see Table 10).

This suggests a sort of continuity in the functions of dreams from childhood into adulthood and/or from early forms to more mature and complex forms of dreaming.

The case of drug dreams, due to their clear relationship with drug craving, provides a good research paradigm for the study *in nature* of the role of motivations in dreams under a magnifying glass. Therefore this research paradigm offers an opportunity to formulate hypotheses about the role of motivational states in dreaming processes.

CHAPTER EIGHT

Drug dreams and Freud's dream theory

C linical observations and systematically collected data show that drug-addicted patients seem to gratify in their dreams, or attempt to do so, their frustrated craving for the drug. From this perspective, several authors have explained drug dreams as a form of wish-fulfilment, with direct reference to Freud's dream theory (Choi, 1973; Colace, 2000b, 2004a; Denzin, 1988, Fiss, 1980; Peters, 2000). Actually, the implications arising from the study of drug dreams with a view to Freud's theory of dreams cover different areas, such as the concepts of drive and desire, the role of desire in triggering dreams, and the issue of the empirical testability of Freud's dream model.

Drug craving and the concept of drive and desire in Freud

The concept of drug craving has been equated to the Freudian concept of drive (Freud, 1915c). This is probably very true for the definition of unconscious drug craving. In Johnson's words: "drives *are* an endogenous force of nature pushing from within that only secondarily come into interaction with the external world" (Johnson, B., 2003b, p. 33). Once the drug craving is established, it will push people to search for drugs, not necessarily with awareness of their desire for such drugs. Shevrin (1997, 2001) suggested that drug craving, as compared to the concept developed by Berridge and Robinson (1995, 1998), has an equivalent in powerful drives in Freud's sense, that is, drives are unconscious and independent from the conscious affective experience and are manifested through "drive derivates". Indeed, in Berridge and Robinson's description (1998), drug craving constitutes an internal pressure or an urgent appetite for drugs that operates unconsciously, including when drugs are unavailable.

Shevrin (2001), too, pointed at the fact that the description of the neural system that mediates drug craving, that is, the "wanting" or "seeking" system (i.e., the mesolimbic–mesocortical DA pathway) (Berridge & Robinson, 1998; Panksepp, 1998) bears much in common with the psychoanalytic concept of drive (for the implications of neuroscience for metapsychology, see also: Johnson, B. 2008a). For example, both Freud's concept of the *source* of drive and the concept of *regulatory imbalances* in Panksepp's SEEKING system refer to states of hunger, thirst, and sex. Freud's concept of drive *pressure* is comparable to what is called, in the SEEKING system, *the states of expectancy or anticipation*. These states exist regardless of the presence of the satisfying object and are a sort of trigger for a variety of goal-seeking behaviours. With regard to this, Shevrin quoted Panksepp and Berridge on the evidence that animals, when in a state of great expectation, act irrationally. For example, if the SEEKING or "wanting" system is activated chemically in a rat, the rat continues to respond to a food-related stimulus even if this is not followed by food. When this system is activated, the rat is satisfied even with a gratifying surrogate object. Shevrin suggested that the human counterpart of this phenomenon refers to Freud's observations of infants, where "... a state of intense craving activates a memory of previous satisfaction that is treated as if it were the satisfaction itself (just as the rat treats the signal as the consummation itself)" (Shevrin, 2001, p. 72).

Furthermore a similar situation is reproduced in the hallucinatory wish-fulfilment of dreams.

Now, I believe that in clinical observations, these concepts are clear in the fact that the upregulated mesolimbic–mesocortical DA system of drug-addicted patients and the consequent onset of drug craving leads them to seek satisfaction of their craving also via the reactivation of a mnestic trace of drugs in their dreams.

I believe that the concept of drug craving, especially in its relation to the concept of hallucinatory satisfaction in dream, closely recalls Freud's first "model of desire" (Freud, 1900a) with its "hydraulic" metaphor, the "constancy principle" (i.e., the psychic apparatus tends to keep excitation at low or constant level), and the concept of "abreaction" (i.e., emotional discharge). Indeed, we know that in Freud's theory of the psychic apparatus (Chapter VII of *The Interpretation of Dreams*) the concept of "desire" and of its mechanism has the same status as the concept of "drive" in later psychic apparatus theories (Greenberg & Mitchell, 1983).

The psychic apparatus, which operates according to the "constancy principle", experiences internal tensions that need to be discharged by means of motoric activity (original real experience of satisfaction). One component of this satisfactory discharge is a perception of the object or situation that has led to satisfaction, and of which a mnestic trace is associated with the excitation produced by the need. So, when the need reappears, the psychic apparatus will attempt to reinvest the perception connected to the original satisfaction: Freud calls this attempt "desire". In this mental conception, the "desire" is the desire to restore something that in the past has satisfied a need (see Greenberg & Mitchell, 1983; Laplanche & Pontalis, 1973).

In these patients, drugs are desirable because they are able to put an end to the internal pressure of drives (i.e., satisfaction). In psychodynamic terms, the satisfaction of drug craving is associated with the use of the drug, the elective object that enables a satisfactory discharge (i.e., the specific action that leads to the obtainment of the adequate object). The desire for the drug originates in this real experience of satisfaction. The mnestic trace of the drug and of its use has an elective value in the constitution of desire. The unavailability of drugs (e.g., in an abstinence state) produces an increase in drug craving, that is, an increase in the internal pressure (intrapsychic tension), accompanied by the onset of drug dreams that enable tension discharge via the hallucinatory fulfilment of the desire for drugs. In Freud's terms, we may view drug dreams as an attempt to reinvest the mnestic trace of the perception of drug (i.e., to set a "perceptual identity"), that provides the original satisfactory discharge of tension.

Drug dreams as the "infantile type" of dreams

The term "infantile" dream, sometimes used by Freud as a synonym for "children's dreams", is a term that designates those types of adult dreams that show the same characteristics as young children's dreams (Freud, 1916–1917, p. 126).

These dreams were also defined as dreams "constructed on infantile lines" (Freud, 1916–1917, p. 134), or dreams showing an "infantile type of fulfilment" (Freud, 1901a, p. 646). These dreams generally appear under conditions of major deprivation of vital needs and/or under unusual living conditions.

> Numerous examples of dreams of this infantile type can be found occurring in adults as well . . . Under unusual or extreme conditions dreams of this infantile character are particularly common. Thus the leader of a polar expedition has recorded that the members of his expedition, while they were wintering in the ice-field and living on a monotonous diet and short rations, regularly dreamt like children of large meals, of mountains of tobacco, and of being back at home. (Freud, 1901a, pp. 645–646)

> In any case, there is yet another class of dreams which are undistorted and, like children's dreams, can easily be recognised as wish-fulfilments. These are the dreams which all through life are called up by imperative bodily needs – hunger, thirst, sexual need – that is, they are wish-fulfilments as reaction to internal somatic stimuli. (Freud, 1916–1917, p. 132)

In adults, these dreams are the only ones in which dream censorship activity is not required and, therefore, the dream content is not distorted or deformed (Freud, 1916–1917, pp. 135, 143). Indeed, from the point of view of the classification of the formal aspects of dreams, infantile dreams are classified as "sensible and intelligible", without surprising and strange elements, compatible with our experiences (Freud, 1901a, pp. 642–643).

Dreams of the infantile type also include the so-called *dreams of convenience*, "in which a person who would like to sleep longer dreams that he is really up and washing himself, or is already at school, whereas he is really still sleeping . . ." (Freud, 1916–1917, pp. 134–135) and the *dreams of impatience*, that is, "if someone has made preparations for a journey, for a theatrical performance that is important to him ... he may dream of a premature fulfilment of his expectation" (p. 134).

In my experience, several drug dreams, in terms of onset, contents, and formal aspects, fall closely into this description of adult dreams of the infantile type. These drug dreams relate to a conscious or preconscious strong desire for the drug. The patients consciously desire a drug and, not being able to use it, they dream about it.

When describing drug dreams, some authors make explicit reference to the Freudian concept of infantile dreams of adults (see Choi, 1973; Colace, 2004a; Makaric, 1979).

Makaric (1979) suggested that alcoholics undergoing alcohol deprivation have frequent infantile dreams about their desire for alcohol.

Choi (1973) reported the following statement by Freud:

> It is easy to prove that dreams often reveal themselves without any disguise as fulfilment of wishes. . . . For instance, there is a dream that I can produce in myself as often as I like—experimentally, as it were. If I eat anchovies or olives or any other highly salted food in the evening, I develop thirst during the night which wakes me up. But my waking is preceded by a dream; and this always has the same content, namely, that I am drinking. I dream I am swallowing down water in great gulps, and it has the delicious state that nothing can equal but a cool drink when one is parched with thirst (Freud, 1900a, p. 123). (Choi, 1973, p. 699)

Starting from this statement, he reported how alcoholics abstinent from drinking dream about drinking more than those who are not abstaining (Choi, 1973).

As in "infantile" dreams of adults, in drug dreams the fulfilment of drug craving is often direct. In some cases the wish-fulfilment that takes place in drug dreams does not reflect in actually using heroin, but merely into pleasantly possessing it, into having a supply of heroin for some later use. Other drug dreams can be understood simply as dreams of anticipation/impatience. In these cases, the dream may be instigated by an increase in drug craving caused by the certainty that the subject will be able to use the drug the next day: in this case, the wish expressed in the dream is something like: "Oh, how I wish it were tomorrow already, so that I could take heroin!" (see the case example).

Case example

A twenty-three-year-old woman, polydrugs dependent (mescaline, LSD, ecstasy/MDMA, benzodiazepine, and amphetamines) reported the following drug dream:

> I was with friends at a rave party, people passed by and offered various drugs. They gave me LSD and I took it. It was a pleasant dream. I woke up disappointed that it was only a dream; I wanted the substance.

The dream was recalled on a Saturday morning. Friday evenings were the moments when the patient experienced the highest degree of craving, because she usually looked forward to going to raves and other parties in the weekend (see Colace, 2010b).

Anguish and distortion in drug dreams

Other drug dreams—less frequent, in my experience—show different characteristics from the "infantile type" described above.

These are drug dreams with a more complex content, in which the fulfilment of the desire to use drugs does not appear clearly. We assume that, in the patients who have these forms of drug dreams, the desire for the drug is unconsciously rejected and disguised in its manifestation in the dream content. Indeed, in these dreams, there is a sort of mild censorship, in various forms. For example, several bizarre circumstances appear that prevent the dreamer from using drugs. (For examples, see Chapter Two.) Other expressions of dream censorship activity might be: (a) *seeing rather than using the drug*, and (b) *certain omissions in dream recall*. In the former case, the patients seem to content themselves with "seeing", instead of culpably "using", the drug; in other words, they select a less guilt-inducing way of interacting with drugs (see Chapter Five). The latter case is a rudimentary form of "dream distortion", which has also been noted in the dreams of older children, when they begin to have dreams similar to those of adults (Colace, 2010a; Freud, 1900a). In other drug dreams, although the desire to use drugs is openly fulfilled, there are anguish and negative feelings, or the dream is interrupted by anxious awakening before drug use occurs.

Both these kinds of drug dreams ("distorted" and "anguishing") are present in those patients who stay drug free for long periods and have changed their lifestyle, succeeding in coping with their drug craving, renouncing drugs; these patients do not view themselves as addicts any more, so the desire for the drug becomes incompatible with their egos and is unconsciously rejected. These drug dreams occur when these patients experience an unconscious, sudden increase in drug craving, perhaps due to the presence in the environment of drug-related cues.

Drug craving as instigator of drug dreams in the perspective of Freud's dream theory

The model of dream formation process in the Freudian theory is formulated especially in "economic" terms (Freud, 1900a, 1905c, 1917d). The dream is apparently formed after a stimulus that threatens to interrupt the sleep that the dream-work would turn into a dream. "In so far as a dream is a reaction to a psychical stimulus, it must be equivalent to dealing with the stimulus in such a way that it is got rid of and that sleep can continue" (Freud, 1916–1917, p. 129).

This is a stimulus that tries to arouse the interest of the sleeper. While, at the moment of going to sleep, the individual loses interest in the elements of the surrounding world, it may happen that certain diurnal residues maintain an interest to the individual that gives rise to the dream: "Observation shows that dreams are instigated by residues from the previous day – thought-cathexes which have not submitted to the general withdrawal of cathexes, but have retained in spite of it a certain amount of libidinal or other interest" (Freud, 1917d, p. 224).

In Freud's view, in order to trigger the dream formation process, a wish must be "strong" enough, in the sense that it must possess an important investment of energy (or of interest) by the sleeper. Generally, in adults, a wish that arose during daytime and remained unsatisfied would not, in itself, attract enough interest to result in a dream without an unconscious ally. However, there are some exceptions to this state of things, where a person's conscious desire alone is sufficiently strong to trigger the dream.

I have never maintained the assertion which has so often been ascribed to me that dream-interpretation shows that all dreams have a sexual content or are derived from sexual motive forces. It is easy to see that hunger, thirst, or the need to excrete, can produce dreams of satisfaction just as well as any repressed sexual or egoistic impulse. The case of young children affords us a convenient test of the validity of our theory of dreams. In them the various psychical systems are not yet sharply divided and the repressions have not yet grown deep, so that we often come upon dreams which are nothing more than undisguised fulfilments of wishful impulses left over from waking life. Under the influence of imperative needs, adults may also produce dreams of this infantile type. (Freud, 1925d, p. 46)

In the perspective of Freud's "economic" viewpoint, the ability of drug craving to trigger drug dreams without an unconscious ally may depend on the abnormal strength that such drug craving has within the psychic apparatus of drug-addicted patients, especially in situations of drug deprivation. Indeed, in drug-addicted patients, the craving for drugs may be even more important than biological drives (hunger and thirst), which we have seen to be sufficient alone to trigger dreams in a Freudian perspective.

Drug dreams and the issue of the empirical testability of Freud's dream theory

We know that Freud used the infantile dreams of adults and children's dreams as a paradigmatic example and, at the same time, an easy piece of evidence for his theory of dreams as wish fulfilment or wish fulfilment attempt (Freud, 1900a, 1933a; on this topic, see Colace, 2009b, 2010a). I believe that this role may also be covered by most drug dreams.

Freud asserted that the frustration of biological or impellent drives increases, in a *correlational sense*, the frequency of dreams undisguisedly (such as infantile dreams) related to it (i.e., the fulfilment or attempted fulfilment of a drive): "On the other hand, dreams of an infantile type seem to occur in adults with special frequency when they find themselves in unusual external circumstances" (Freud, 1900a, p. 131, fn. 1).

The study of the frequency of drug dreams after drug craving frustration has an empirical probative relevance for this Freudian hypothesis. Indeed, on the basis of the Freudian model, we should expect an increase in the frequency of these dreams just as a result of drug deprivation. Furthermore, although drug dreams are not a direct test for the general assumption that all dreams represent a wish fulfilment or a wish-fulfilment attempt, they do have a certain probative relevance for this. Since Freud considered infantile dreams to be the "simplest case" in support of his main hypothesis, if systematic studies showed that even in this "blatant theoretical condition" there are no frequent wish fulfilment or wish-fulfiment attempt dreams, this would represent a fact unambiguously contrary to his general assumption, because it would prove that *at least some dreams are not a fulfilment of a wish*. From this point of view, studies on drug dreams gain relevance when it comes to assessing the validity of Freud's theory of dreams and, more importantly, they prove that this theory is empirically testable. Incidentally, this indicates, as already happened in other occasions, that Freud's assumptions are, in principle, falsifiable according to the Popperian framework (Popper, 1959; 1963) (see: Colace, 2010a, 2013; Grünbaum, 1984; Guénole, Marcaggi, & Baleyte, 2013; Solms, 1997) (see Box 6).

The researchers with knowledge of Freud's dream theory may easily observe that drug dreams, like other infantile dreams, come into play for the purpose of testing the validity of the following Freudian assumptions:

● dreams are valid and meaningful psychic acts, since they are a finalised (and not random) act [i.e., the fulfilment of wish] (Freud, 1901a, p. 643; 1916–1917, pp. 127–128);
● not all dreams represent a fulfilment of repressed sexual wishes (Freud, 1925d, p. 46);
● not all dreams are bizarre (Freud, 1901a, pp. 642–643, 1916–1917, p. 143);
● dream distortion is not intrinsic to the nature of dream processes (Freud, 1910a, p. 34; 1916–1917, p. 128);
● dream is the guardian of sleep (Freud, 1916–1917, p. 129);
● Dreams are a psychic "safety valve" for instinctual drives (Freud, 1900a, p. 579).

Conclusions

In my view, at present, Freud's theory of dream represents a good conceptual framework for the comprehension of drug dreams. It

Box 6.   The issue of the empirical untestability of Freud's dream theory

Except for some recent scientific contributions (Solms, 1995, 1997, 2000) that have led us to reconsider sizeable parts of Freud's dream theory and revived the dream debate (Boag, 2006a,b; Domhoff, 2001, 2005; Hobson, 2000, 2004, 2005, 2006; Solms, 2004, 2006), authors have frequently claimed that Freud's dream theory does not have empirical properties and credentials and would not be empirically testable (e.g., Domhoff, 2001, 2005; Hobson, 1988, 2002, 2013; Hobson, Pace-Schott, & Stickgold, 2000; Valli, 2008; Vogel, 2000). For example, Hobson attributed three vital defects to the psychoanalytic theory of dream. First, this theory "is not scientific because it is not empirically based" (Hobson, 1988, p. 53). Second, "the psychoanalytic theory is not logically constructed in such a way as to make it amenable to direct experimental test" (Hobson, 1988, p. 53), and it does not allow either quantitative observations or exact predictions (p. 55). Third, "psychoanalysts have never even defined the sort of evidence that could refute the theory" (Hobson, 1988, pp. 53–54). Actually, various areas of research (i.e., neuropsychology of dream (Solms, 1997, 2000), childrens' dreams (Colace, 2010a, 2013), biological drive frustration paradigm (Bokert, 1968), and others (see, for example, the recent study on dreams as the guardians of sleep: Guénole, Marcaggi, and Baleyte (2013)) show that the Freudian hypotheses about dreams are empirically testable, as mentioned earlier for its clinical aetiologic hypotheses (Grünbaum, 1984, p. 110). All these studies suggest that various parts of Freud's dream theory have an extraordinary heuristic value. For example, I have pointed out elsewhere, through the study of children's dreams, that several components of the theory of dreams are potentially empirically testable, including some very important issues such as the wish fulfilment hypothesis, the dream censorship model, etc. (Colace, 2009c; 2010a, 2011, 2012, 2013).

provides us with the theoretical constructs for understanding the mechanism of the onset and formation processes of these dreams, their contents, their psychological function and their clinical usefulness (Figure 4).

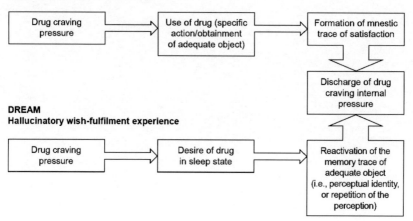

Figure 4. The drug dream process in the Freudian perspective.

CHAPTER NINE

Drug dreams and the neuropsychoanalytic model of dreams

Neuropsychoanalysis analyses the "... internal psychological structure of the various changes in personality, motivations and complex emotions that occur following a damage to different cerebral structures" (Kaplan-Solms & Solms, 2000, p. 62) (see also Solms & Turnbull, 2002; 2011). One of the most important applications of this approach is the study of the dreaming process (Solms, 1997). In this chapter, I shall describe how the study of drug dreams might contribute to prove the validity of neuropsychoanalytic findings concerning the dreaming process. In fact, drug dreams represent a real exemplification and, at the same time, a clinical support to Solms's neuropsychological model.

The neuropsychoanalytic model of dream

Neuropsychological studies on dreaming are based on the observation of subjects who, due to a lesion in a specific brain area, have changed their way of dreaming. These studies suggest which brain structures are involved in the ordinary process of dreaming, that is, the cerebral organisation of dreaming (Solms, 1995, 1997, 2000, 2011).

I shall summarise here only the findings from Solms's studies that are useful with a view to discussing drug dreams.

Solms found that a group of patients affected by a lesion in the pontine brainstem, an anatomical region considered crucial for the regulation of REM sleep state, could preserve their dreaming activity, while an overall cessation of dreaming was observed in another group of patients who had suffered focal lesions that involved (a) a parieto–temporo–occipital junction (i.e., cognitive process involved in mental imagery, memory deficit, etc.), or (b) a bilateral frontal lobe lesion. These findings led Solms to conclude that the brain parts that are crucial for dreaming and those that are crucial for REM sleep are anatomically and functionally separated.

More or less concurrently with Solms's observations, the functional neuroimaging studies also demonstrated that the dreaming process involves several forebrain structures, including the frontal and limbic areas (i.e., anterior and lateral hypothalamic areas, amygdaloid complex, septal–ventral striatal areas, orbitofrontal and anterior cingulate cortices, entorhinal and insular areas) and occipito–temporal cortical areas (Braun et al., 1997; Maquet et al., 1996; Nofzinger, Mintun, Wiseman, Kupfer, & Moore, 1997). Furthermore, Solms's findings were substantiated by other subsequent studies (Bischof & Bassetti, 2004; Jakobson, Fitzgerald, & Conduit, 2012; Oudiette et al., 2012; Yu, 2007) (see Box 7).

According to Solms's conclusions, the part of the brain involved as "primary generator" of dreaming is the white matter surrounding the frontal horn of the lateral ventricles (i.e., the ventromesial quadrant of frontal lobes) (Figure 5). This part of the brain accommodates the mesolimbic–mesocortical dopamine pathways (ML–MC DA) that arise from the cell group of the ventral tegmental area and project toward the limbic and frontal structures. The ML–MC DA pathways are described by affective neuroscience as the core of the "SEEKING" system, the instigator of goal-seeking behaviour and of appetitive interactions with the world (Panksepp, 1998). This are also described as a "wanting" system (Robinson & Berridge, 1993, Berridge & Robinson, 1998).

As Solms noticed, his clinico–anatomical findings match with some previous neurological and psychiatric observations on the general cessation of dreaming in correlation with focal forebrain lesion (on the parieto–temporo–occipital junction and ventro-mesial quadrant of the frontal lobe) and following prefrontal leucotomy (for a review, see Solms, 1997, 2000).

Box 7.   Recent studies that are consistent with Solms

Bischof & Bassetti (2004) have described the case of a seventy-three-year-old woman who reported total dream loss after acute bilateral occipital artery infarction (including the right inferior lingual gyrus) while still preserving REM sleep, as demonstrated by polysomnography.

Yu (2007) largely replicated Solms's findings about an association between dream cessation and lesions to the ventromesial frontal region in patients who were diagnosed with infarction. Furthermore, Yu found that, compared with the other neural components in the ventromesial frontal pathway, the role of the caudate nucleus appeared to be particularly salient in the functional architecture of dreaming.

Jakobson, Fitzgerald, and Conduit (2012), using a novel brain stimulation technique, showed that transcranial direct current stimulation, applied simultaneously to the frontal and right posterior parietal cortex during NREM stage 2 sleep, produced an increase in the frequency of dream reports with visual imagery. The authors concluded that this result was due to a general arousing effect and/or reproduction of a cortical neural activity similar to that involved in dreaming.

Oudiette and colleagues (2012) showed that long and bizarre dreams persist even after partial or total suppression of REM sleep (achieved by means of clomipramine 50 mg) and suggested that the generation of mental activity during sleep is independent from REM sleep stage.

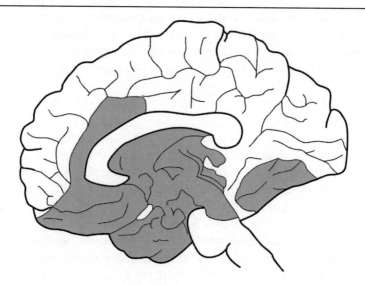

Figure 5.   The dreaming brain (adapted from Solms & Turnbull, 2002).

In Solms's perspective, all the brain states that are correlated with dreaming imply cerebral activation during sleep. Now, the high correlation between dreaming and REM state is based on the fact that REM sleep state is the most common source of cerebral activation during sleep. However, the cerebral activation during REM sleep is not sufficient for the triggering of dreams. Dreaming occurs only when a cerebral activation engages the ML–MC DA system (Solms, 2000).

Solms suggested that dream activity can be switched "on" or "off" by switching "on" or "off" ML–MC DA activity (Solms, 2000, p. 847), and this converges with the results of studies on the neuropharmacology of dreaming. It has been observed that the dopamine agonists that act in the ML–MC DA system cause an increase in the dreaming process. For example, doses of L-DOPA determine a strong increase in dream frequency and vividness (Hartmann, Russ, Oldfield, Falke, & Skoff, 1980; Massetani, Lucchetti, Piccini, & Bianchi, 1986; Moscovitz, Moses, & Klawans, 1978; Nausieda, Weiner, Kaplan, Weber, & Klawans, 1982). Conversely, drugs such as antipsychotics, which block dopamine transmission in the ML–MC system (e.g., haloperidol) inhibit the dreaming activity (Gaillard & Moneme, 1977; Sacks, 1985, 1990). For example, Gaillard and Moneme (1977) showed that sulpiride (a blocker of dopamine receptors in the mesolimbic/mesocortical dopaminergic system), compared to placebo conditions, decreased the number of dreams with high scores in verbal aggression, physical aggression, and sexuality. In the authors' view, this result supports the correlation between the ML–MC DA system and the expression of emotions and drives in dreams.

Solms also pointed out that the neuropsychological findings are compatible with the Freudian dream theory, and, in particular, with Freud's assertion that dreams are instigated by wishes (Solms, 2000). Indeed, the fact that the "SEEKING" system, the most important structure involved in triggering dreams, is also responsible for biological motivations is consistent with Freud's idea that ". . . dreams give expression to instinctual drive" (Solms, 2000, p. 619). On the other hand, the "SEEKING" system is active in appetitive states and is also associated with terms like "curiosity" or "interest", which closely recall Freud's concept of "libido" (a term that neurobiologists have replaced with "appetite") and with its role in triggering dreams, according to the Freudian model.

Finally, two important corollaries of neuropsychological findings on dreams are the following: (a) dreams can hardly be considered as mere epiphenomena of neurobiological events of REM sleep state, or the result of random processes (Hobson, 1988), (b) the Freudian model of dreams is, in principle, empirically testable, even outside a psychoanalytic setting.

The neuropsychoanalytic hypothesis of drug dreams

As B. Johnson (2001) pointed out, drug dreams may be viewed, in the perspective of a neuropsychoanalytic approach, as an alteration of normal dreaming processes (drug dreams do not occur in healthy people) caused by persistent changes in the neurological functions due to prolonged drug exposure. Solms also underlined that dopaminergic activation in drug-addicted patients who crave the drug is a real example of what he meant by dopaminergic activation in dreams. In fact, with reference to these areas of the brain, he wrote, ". . . we know that that part of the brain becomes highly active when an addict is seeking out the substance that he or she is addicted to" (Solms, 1999, p. 2).

B. Johnson (2001) was the first to try to integrate the findings of neuropsychology of dreams with those of the neurobiology of addiction, by formulating the "neuropsychoanalytic hypothesis" of drug dreams. His original contribution lies in having pointed out that the mesolimbic–mesocortical dopaminergic system, identified by Solms's neuropsychological studies as essential in the generation of dreaming, is exactly the one that, when upregulated by an exposure to addictive drugs, is responsible for drug craving (Robinson & Berridge, 1993, see Chapter Three) and the related drug dreams (see also Johnson, B., 2003a, 2008b, 2012).

Johnson's conclusion that "drug addiction provides an important 'experiment of nature' regarding drives and dreaming" (Johnson, B., 2001, p. 93), where drug dreams are due to the neurological changes produced by drug exposure, is a very interesting starting point for a neuropsychoanalytical approach to the study of drug dreams and of the vicissitudes of drug craving, viewed as a new drive in Freudian sense.

A neuropsychoanalytic approach to drug dreams: the measure of changes in the limbic activity among drug-addict patients in relation to drug dreaming

We have seen how the mesolimbic–mesocortical DA circuits (ML–MC DA) are the key brain sites that mediate the effects of drugs and the onset of drug craving. When exposed repeatedly to drugs, these circuits are sensitised and upregulated. The mesolimbic–mesocortical DA circuit includes projections from the cell bodies of the ventral tegmentum to the limbic structures, in particular in the nucleus accumbens, anterior cingulate cortex, amygdaloid complex, and dorsolateral prefrontal cortex (Panksepp, 1998; Solms & Turnbull, 2002; Alcaro, Huber, & Panksepp, 2007).

Actually, limbic system irritability, as measured by means of a symptoms scale suggesting temporal lobe epilepsy (TLE), such as the Limbic System Check List (LSCL-33: Teicher, Glod, Surrey, & Swett, 1993; see Box 8) or the Complex Partial Seizure-like Symptoms Inventory (CPSI) (Roberts et al., 1992), has been observed in alcoholic patients (Jasova, Bob, & Fedor-Freybergh, 2007; Bob, Jasova, Bizik, & Raboch, 2011), in heroin-addicted patients (Colace 2009a; Colace, Belsanti, & Antermite, n.d.; Colace et al., 2010), and in smoker students (Světlák, Bob, & Kukleta, 2010). Furthermore, LSCL scores were found to be in statistically significant correlation with alcohol craving (Bob, Jasova, Bizik, & Raboch, 2011; Jasova, Bob, & Fedor-Freybergh, 2007) and with substance abuse among college students (Anderson, Teicher, Polcari, & Renshaw, 2002).

Box 8.   The Limbic System Checklist

The Limbic System Checklist, LSCL-33 (Teicher, Glod, Surrey, & Swett, 1993) is a thirty-three-item self-reported questionnaire designed to measure limbic system dysfunction. It was originally devised to ascertain the frequency of somatic, sensory, behavioural, and memory symptoms suggestive of temporal lobe epilepsy (e.g., dissociative disturbance, automatism, paroxysmal somatic disturbances, etc.). Subjects rated the frequency of symptoms using a four-point Likert scale (never = 0, rarely = 1, sometimes = 2, often = 4). The LSCL-33 shows psychometric properties and internal consistency (Cronbach's alpha 0.90) well. The subjects with temporal lobe epilepsy reported high scores (range 23–60), while normal adults reported scores < 10. LSCL-33 is correlated with other measures of limbic dysfunction (e.g., the Hopkins Symptom Checklist) (Teicher, Glod, Surrey, & Swett, 1993).

Drug-addicted patients reported high LSCL-33 scores. In particular, heroin-addicted patients reported mean total scores in the range of 23–27 (Colace, Belsanti, & Antermite, n.d.; Colace et al. 2010) and alcoholic patients reported a LSCL-33 mean total score of 31.9 (Jasova, Bob, & Fedor-Freybergh, 2007). Furthermore, drug-addicted subjects reported higher LSCL-33 scores compared to occasional drug abusers (cocaine and/or cannabis) with no diagnosis of drug addiction (Colace et al., 2010) and to healthy individuals (Anderson, Teicher, Polcari, & Renshaw, 2002; Jasova, Bob, & Fedor-Freybergh, 2007). It is plausible to interpret the limbic system irritability showed by drug-addict subjects as a direct expression of the upregulation of mesolimbic–mesocortical dopamine (DA) circuits due to prolonged drug exposure.

Under a neuropsychoanalytic perspective, recent studies have investigated the possibility to measure the change in ML-MC DA circuits in drug-addicted patients via the Limbic System Check List, also in relation to their drug dream activity (Colace, 2009a; Colace, et al., 2010; Colace, Belsanti & Antermite, n.d.). Indeed, while various studies admitted the relationship between the upregulation of this limbic DA circuit and the onset of drug craving and drug dreams, they did not include any direct or indirect measure of mesolimbic-mesocortical DA neural activity, nor of the limbic system functioning of drug-addicted subjects who reported drug dreams. These studies demonstrate that the *same* group of drug-addicted patients who reported drug dreams showed irritability of the limbic system (Colace, 2009a; Colace et al., 2010; Colace, Belsanti & Antermite, n.d.). Vice-versa, occasional drug users (i.e., with no diagnosis of drug dependence or the presence of drug craving) did not report *neither limbic irritability nor drug dreams* (Colace et al., 2010). This result suggested that limbic irritability in drug-addicted subjects seems to be the neurobiological background in which drug dreams may occur, although other drug-addicted subjects with a similar limbic system tone may not have such dreams (Colace et al. 2010).

We note that the association between limbic hyperfunction and the occurrence of dreams in drug-addicted subjects provides another converging line of evidence with Solms's findings about the active role of the mesolimbic–mesocortical dopaminergic system (i.e., the "seeking" or "wanting" system) in the motivational triggering of dream processes (Solms, 1997, 2000). The limbic irritability in drug dreaming matches with the data in literature where subjects with epileptiform activity in the temporal lobe reported recurrent non-REM dreams with a strong emotional connotation (e.g., recurrent nightmares) (for a review, see Solms, 1997, 2000). Furthermore, other studies show that limbic hyperfunction, measured with LSCL-33, predicts objective threat-related dreams (Peterson, Henke, & Hayes (2002) and that motivational and emotional contents are significantly more present in the dream reports collected after REM-sleep awakening, in which limbic areas are known to be more active, than in those after non-REM-sleep awakening (Smith et al., 2004).

A "dopaminergic" hypothesis about drug-dream onset

Data from various areas of study, and in particular from the neurobiology of drug craving, the neuropsychology of dream, the clinics of drug dreams, and the phenomenology of drug dreams, as well as the recent studies of limbic system dysfunction in drug-addict patients, allow for the formulation of a "dopaminergic hypothesis" about the onset of drug dreams (Colace, 2007, 2009a; Colace et al., 2010).

Background evidence

The data relevant to this hypothesis are summarised below in the following points.

1. In drug-addict patients, drug exposure produces an upregulation of the ML–MC dopaminergic system through the mechanism of sensitisation, which results in a greater increase in dopaminergic activity in response to a drug-conditioned cues and in the onset of drug craving (Berridge & Robinson, 1998; Robinson & Berridge, 1993; Wise, 2004) (see Chapter Three for details).
2. Functional neuroimaging studies have shown that when drug-addicted patients experience a strong desire for drugs there is an increase in ML–MC DA firing at the neurobiological level (Goldstein et al., 2009; Gorelick et al., 2005; Volkow et al., 2006; Wong et al., 2006).
3. Studies have shown that during abstinence from drugs there is greater vulnerability to drug-conditioned cues and acute drug

craving episodes are more likely to occur (Di Chiara, 1996; Koob, 2011; Stinus, Le Moal, & Koob, 1990).

4.   Studies on dreaming in addiction have shown that the appearance of drug dreams is related to drug-craving intensification during abstinence (Choi, 1973; Colace, 2000b, 2004a, 2006; Christo & Franey, 1996; Fiss, 1980). In contrast, drug dreams more rarely occur when the subjects are using the drug regularly (Choi, 1973; Hajek & Belcher, 1991; Persico, 1992; for a review, see Colace, 2004a).

5.   Solms's neuropsychological studies (1997, 2000; see also Yu, 2007) have shown that the activation of the ML–MC DA system (i.e., the SEEKING or "Wanting" system) is the "primary generator" of dreaming.

6.   Other converging lines of evidence show that dopaminergic agents increase the frequency of dreaming and that the "dream-on mechanism" is dopaminergic (see above).

A dopaminergic hypothesis

On the basis of the data above, we may describe a theoretical situation in which drug dreams appear. In drug-addicted subjects who crave for drugs (not necessarily being aware of it) there is an increase in ML–MC DA release levels. In a normal situation, that is, while the patients are regularly using their drugs, this DA level is "discharged" after the use of drugs, and then the baseline DA levels are re-established (i.e., drug craving satisfaction). At this stage, drug dreams rarely appear. Conversely, in a condition of abstinence from drugs or abrupt cessation or unavailability of the drug, the patients experience a more intense drug craving (i.e., amplification of the motivational impact of drug-conditioned cues, greater vulnerability to drug-conditioned cues), and have a greater DA release, which are not followed by the use of the drug and, therefore, DA levels are not "discharged": this is the condition in which drug dreams are more likely to appear. In summary: *in a condition of already upregulated ML–MC DA system, in a phase highly vulnerable to drug-conditioned cues, due to abstinence from drugs, drug dream onset is instigated by a temporary increase of DA release "not discharged"* (Colace, 2007; 2009a; Colace, Belsanti, & Antermite, n.d.; Colace et al., 2010) (Figure 6).

Conclusions

We have seen that, acccording to a neuropsychoanalytic approach, the activation of the MC–ML dopaminergic system is the "dream-on mechanism".

Now, drug dreams may be considered as a specific case of this mechanism. In fact, we have seen that an increase in DA release/drug craving is closely related with the onset of dreams reflecting such a motivational state (i.e., drug craving).

Thus, the study of drug dreams is found to be particularly appropriate to show the dopaminergic activation of dreaming and the role of the brain areas involved in basic motivations in the process of dreaming.

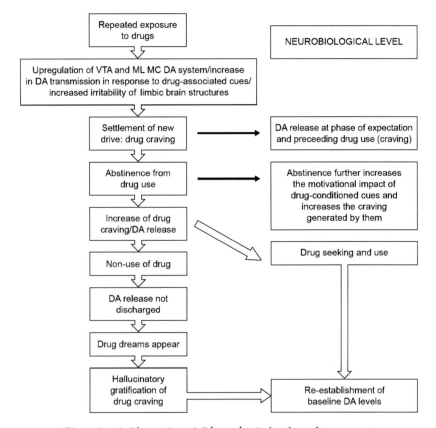

Figure 6.   A "dopaminergic" hypothesis for drug dream onset.

CHAPTER TEN

Conclusion and research agenda

The study of drug dreams has shown important implications for both the clinics and therapy of addiction rather than for general dream research and theory. It is, therefore, advisable to continue investigating this phenomenon.

At present, although the number of systematic studies on the topic is not yet sufficient and even seems to be imbalanced in favour of certain drugs rather than others, the results obtained make it possible to sketch a first overview of this phenomenon with some firm points.

Drug dreams are a phenomenon typical and exclusive of drug-addicted patients who, typically, show a craving for drugs. They do not occur in people who do not use substances and in those who use drugs occasionally. These dreams are a significant expression of drug craving, or, better said, of a high degree of drug craving. This is the reason why drug dreams appear mainly during periods of abstinence from drugs, when the intensity of the drug craving increases, and are much less present during the periods when patients use drugs regularly.

The phenomenology of drug dreams is the same across the different types of addiction. In alcoholics, heroin-addicted patients, cocaine-addicted patients, tobacco-smoking patients, and other types of dependencies, drug dreams often involve the dreamer who uses or attempts to use the drug of abuse feeling completely similar emotions in dreams (e.g., pleasure/urge, guilt, fear) and upon awakening (disappointment or relief when the patient realises that no actual use of the substance was made). These dreams occur more as an expression of drug craving than of the desire to stay clean. Indeed, drug dreams rarely have content about an explicit rejection of the drug.

The analysis of drug dreams is favoured by the fact that these, contrary to what happens to the ordinary dreams of adults, are often directly understandable with respect to the patient's experiences. From this point of view, they represent valuable psychic material for all therapists (i.e., counsellors, psychotherapists, psychologists, psychiatrists, clinicians) involved in the treatment of drug-addicted patients. Through drug dreams, it is possible to have access to the drug craving of the patients, to its current intensity, to the patients' ability to cope with it, to the psychological issues that they imply for the patients, alongside the progress of the therapy and/or the changes experienced by the patients. Drug dreams are always ready to reveal the sudden increase in drug craving (that is sometimes only unconscious) and might sometimes warn us of a potential impending relapse of the patient. The frequency of drug dreams (increase/decrease) can also give us indications on the effectiveness of the anti-craving action of the medications for drug addiction.

Although the authors unanimously acknowledge the clinical and therapeutic usefulness of drug dreams, it is equally clear that much remains to be done in order to exploit such usefulness. I believe that the collection of drug dreams should be included in the routine clinical and therapeutic protocols for drug-addicted patients, and that therapists should use these dreams in a more active and informed way, for example, by monitoring the changes in their frequency, or in their content. Furthermore, I have proposed here some specific clinical actions in response to sudden appearance of drug dreams, to the variation of their frequency, and in relation to their contents and emotions (e.g., management of guilt, monitoring of drug craving, management of fear of relapsing, etc.).

The patients themselves, through drug dreams, could develop a greater awareness of their problem and their current situation with respect to drugs and should, therefore, be encouraged to write down their drug dreams and report them to their therapist.

Beyond their clinical functions, drug dreams certainly also have important individual adaptive psychological functions. These are functions already identified for dreams in general in different research areas (see, for example, the theories on the emotional adaptive functions of dreams), and that appear even more clearly in drug dreams. These dreams enable a "discharge" of drug craving pressure (i.e., a safe way) through its hallucinatory fulfilment, they help to develop strategies for coping with drug craving, and they are an alert signal that the drug addiction is not resolved. More generally, drug dreams allow the patients to get in touch with those parts of their self that are ill (addiction) and those that are healthy. And on the other side, drug dreams have some influence on the psychological state of the patients in the post-dream reality, in particular on the extent of their drug craving and their degree of vulnerability to relapse. Therefore, sometimes these dreams are true warning signs that patients should learn to grasp and report to their therapist.

At present, the indications about using drug dreams for prognostic purposes are still insufficient and not always consistent. This problem calls for a phenomenological study of these dreams that might identify and describe their contents, the emotions felt during the dreams and upon awakening, cross-referenced across all the various types of drug addiction, in order to highlight the various types of drug dreams and their different prognostic significance. Not all drug dreams are the same, and might have different prognostic meanings.

In my opinion, a possible interpretation of drug dreams for the purpose of their prognostic use is presently represented by the evaluation of whether or not the drug is used successfully in the dream. In general, the ability to suggest a favourable prognosis in the short term lies in the ability to understand whether the dream is able to perform its function of drug craving satisfaction. When the dream is gratifying, the patient will be able to remain abstinent when awake. Conversely, when the dream could not perform its gratification function, there may be a danger of greater drug craving, with the risk of a relapse, unless treated.

However, there is a case in which the predictive meaning of drug dreams allows for an easier reading: some drug dreams, particularly those that appear after a long period of non-use of substances, often indicate a sudden increase in the patient's drug craving (sometimes only unconscious) and, therefore, his/her greater vulnerability to its possible consequences. When these dreams occur, the clinician must make sure that all the situations that could further increase drug craving and endanger the patient are kept under control.

*   *   *

Although the studies on drug dreams were born in a predominantly clinical and therapeutic context, this book has tried to show how it would be useful and appropriate to use drug dreams as a research paradigm for the study of dreams in general and, in particular, for the purpose of investigating the role of basic motivations in the dreaming process. From this point of view, I believe that the drug dreams may be of interest also for sleep and dream researchers.

Drug dreams are a typical example of dreams that arise as a result of the deprivation of an important urge of the individual. Their goal is to fulfil or attempt to fulfil the desire to use the drug, and they reproduce a situation similar to the one that is had with the dreams that arise as a the result of biological drive frustration. In other words, drug deprivation increases drug craving, which generates dreams about drug use, in the same way as food deprivation increases hunger, which generates dreams about eating.

Drug craving presents the same high level of intensity and indefeasibility as biological drives, and also the same neurobiological substrate, since both are mediated by the ML–MC DA system. The study of the effects of biological drive frustration on dream contents, already many years before the advent of lesion studies and neuroimaging studies of dreaming, had proved to be important for the investigation of the motivational determinants of dreaming. However, for unclear reasons, they did not gain much following. With this book, I am proposing that drug dreams can be a stimulus for, and also a continuation of, this research paradigm.

The clinics and phenomenology of drug dreams clearly show that these dreams are motivationally determined and that they serve a motivational function, such as that of "discharging" the drug craving pressure (i.e., a safe way function or drive regulation function). For this reason, these dreams are an important theoretical and clinical phenomenon with regard to the theories about dream in general and on the role of motivations in the process of dreaming. For example, drug dreams are consistent with recent hypothesis according to which the reactivation in sleep of memories of high emotional and motivational value for the dreamer has an important role in the construction of the dream (see Chapter Seven). Such "discharge" functions are also consistent with recent studies on the role of sleep and dream in the "dissipation" of the dreamer's previous-day emotional charge (see Chapter Seven).

On the other hand, drug dreams clash with the theories that see dreams as motivationally neutral phenomena, as epiphenomena, based mainly on PGO random activation during sleep state.

Again, with regard to the role of motivation in dreaming, different authors have shown that most drug dreams are consistent with the theory of dream that, more than any other, underlined the deep motivational origin of dreaming: that is, the Freudian theory. In fact, drug dreams are often a fulfilment of the wish to use drugs. In my view, many drug dreams fall within Freud's classic description of adult dreams "constructed on infantile lines" (1900a). In fact, in many drug dreams, this fulfilment is clear and direct and in this respect these dreams are similar to other forms of infantile dreams, such as those described above, triggered by the frustration of biological drives or other urgent needs, and those recalled by young children. From this point of view, drug dreams, as already shown by other forms of childhood dreams, provide an effective test bench for various hypotheses of Freud's theory of dream, and disprove the thesis—widespread in the scientific community—of the alleged empirical untestability of this model.

I believe that the most important thing, however, is the fact that several Freudian concepts, such as the first model of desire, some important general principles of the psychic apparatus, and the dream model itself, seem to constitute a conceptual theoretical framework that can describe and explain consistently the mechanism of initiation, the process, the phenomenology, and the psychological and individual significance of drug dreams: all this proves the heuristic value and the vitality of the Freudian model of dreaming.

Drug dreams can have an equally important strategic value in respect of the most recent neuropsychoanalytic investigation on dreaming. In fact, it has been noted that drug dreams are an example *in nature* of what was proved by these studies to be the primary mechanism involved in the generation of dreams: that is, the activation of ML–MC DA pathways, the core of the so called SEEKING system.

Generally, the activation of this system through an increase in dopamine release causes a higher frequency and greater vividness of dreams. Now, the activation of the SEEKING system is considered "non-specific" because the "SEEKING" system is activated in the same way for different types of drives. However, the "SEEKING" system is associated with memory systems that indicate what "object" will satisfy our need (based on learning from experience) and should, therefore, be sought in the outside world. In the case of drug-addicted patients, the upregulation of ML–MC DA pathways provides the anatomical substrate of drug craving and, at the same time, of drug dreams.

Furthermore, recent indications provide evidence of an actual increased irritability of the limbic system in addicted patients, and at least two studies show that patients who have drug dreams also present an increased irritability of the limbic system. From this point of view, I believe that drug dreams are a clinical and theoretical example of dopaminergic activation of dreaming, which is consistent with the neuropsychoanalytic model of dream.

The set of data primarily related to the neurobiology of drug addiction and drug craving, and those on the role of dopamine in the instigation of dreaming in general, has led me to sketch a dopaminergic hypothesis about drug dream onset. In particular, I speculated that drug dream onset is instigated by a temporary increase in DA release "not discharged" as neurobiological substrate of the drug craving increases.

It is, therefore, clear that the drug dream phenomenon might be helpful in assessing the knowledge from various field of research (therapies of addiction, neurobiology of addiction, affective neuroscience, dream research and theories, neuropsychoanalysis) that these dreams summarise together.

In conclusion, what the study of drug dreams suggests is their desirable systematic use in the clinical practice, and their profitable study for those dream and sleep researchers who are interested in investigating how motivational states affect dreaming. In the following pages I have tried to draw up a research agenda that I hope will earn positive response (Box 9).

Box 9.   Research agenda

Improve drug dream reports reliability by collecting them as close as possible to the dream experience. For example, in patients living in the therapeutic community, drug dream reports might be collected immediately upon awakening through a systematic interview.

Investigate the time needed for the first onset of drug dreams with respect to the date when patient started using drugs.

Investigate the prevalence of drug dreams in different types of drug addiction with respect to age and gender.

Conduct a systematic phenomenological analysis of drug dream content (general content, and emotions during the dream and upon awakening) on a large sample of drug-addicted patients.

Study the frequencies of the various types of drug dreams: infantile drug dreams, anxious drug dreams, and those drug dreams that may present symbolic and more complex content.

Observe the differences between the drug dreams that occur during the early period of abstinence and those that arise after a long period of abstinence following a sudden recrudescence of craving.

Compare the prognostic significance of the different types of drug dreams, especially those about successful drug use and those about failed drug use.

A selective bilateral lesion of the globus pallidus causes the patient's total loss of drug craving (i.e., craving disappears). From this point of view, it would be interesting to see whether drug dreams, too, disappear or not in these patients.

Study systematically the effects of different pharmacological treatments (agonists and antagonists) and of their different dosage in the onset of drug dreams and/or their frequency.

Based on the results achieved in various clinical settings, draw up guidelines on the clinical actions that the therapist might adopt when a patient reports drug dreams, according to the content and meaning of these.

Identify more accurate experimental patterns for studying the cause–effect role of drug craving in the instigation of drug dreams. For example, study the frequency of drug dreams in the period that follows a systematic induction of drug craving through the use of drug-related cues.

Study the effects of unaware drug craving stimulation on the frequency of drug dreams.

Study the effects of the phobic component of craving compared with the appetitive–desiderative component in the onset and/or increased frequency of drug dreams.

Study systematically the effects of the various types of drug dreams on the intensity of drug craving upon awakening from the dream and in the days following it.

REFERENCES

AA.VV. (1995). *Il Messaggero*, 30 September, Rome.

AA.VV. (2000). *Il Messagero*, 29 January, Rome.

Addolorato, G., Caputo, F., Capristo, E., Domenicali, M., Bernardi M., Janiri L., Agabio, R., Colombo, G., Gessa, G. L., & Gasbarrini, G. (2002). Baclofen efficacy in reducing alcohol craving and intake: a preliminary double-blind randomized controlled study. *Alcohol and Alcoholism, 37*(5): 504–508.

Alcaro, A., & Panksepp, J. (2011). The SEEKING mind: primal neuro-affective substrates for appetitive incentive states and their pathological dynamics in addictions and depression. *Neuroscience and Biobehavioral Reviews, 35*(9): 1805–1820.

Alcaro, A., Huber, R., & Panksepp, J. (2007). Behavioral functions of the mesolimbic dopaminergic system: an affective neuroethological perspective. *Brain Research Reviews, 56*: 283–321.

Alcoholics Anonymous World Services (1975). *Living Sober*. New York: Dolphin Books.

Ameisen, O. (2005). Complete and prolonged suppression of symptoms and consequences of alcohol-dependence using high-dose Baclofen: a self-case report of a physician. *Alcohol & Alcoholism, 40*(2): 147–150.

American Psychiatric Association (1994). *Diagnostic and Statistical Manual of Mental Disorders* (4th edn). Washington, DC: APA.

Andersen, R. S. (1975). Operation Homecoming: psychological observation of repatriated Vietnam prisoners of war. *Psychiatry, 38*: 65–74.

Anderson, C. M., Teicher, M. H., Polcari, A., & Renshaw, P. F. (2002). Abnormal T2 relaxation time in the cerebellar vermis of adults sexually abused in childhood: potential role of the vermis in stress-enhanced risk for drug abuse. *Psychoneuroendocrinology, 27*: 232-244.

Antrobus, J. S. (2001). Rethinking the fundamental processes of dream and sleep mentation production: defining new questions that avoid the distraction of REM versus NREM comparison. *Sleep and Hypnosis, 3*: 1–3.

Aragona, B. J., Liu, Y., Yu, Y. J., Curtis, J. T., Detwiler, J. M., Insel, T. R., & Wang, Z. (2006). Nucleus accumbens dopamine differentially mediates the formation and maintenance of monogamous pair bonds. *Nature Neuroscience, 9*: 133–139.

Araujo, R. B., Oliveira, M., Piccoloto, L. B., & Szupszynski, K. (2004). Sonhos e craving em alcoolistas na fase de desintoxicação [Dreams and craving in alcohol addicted patients in the detoxication stage]. *Revista Psiqiatria Clinica, 31*(2): 63–69.

Arkin, A. M., & Antrobus, J. S. (1991). The effects of external stimuli applied prior to and during sleep on sleep experience. In: A. M. Arkin, J. S. Antrobus, & S. J. Ellman (Eds.), *The Mind in Sleep: Psychology and Psychophysiology* (pp. 265–307). Hillsdale, NJ: Lawrence Erlbaum.

Arkin, A. M., & Steiner, S. S. (1978). The effects of drugs on sleep mentation. In: A. M. Arkin, J. S. Antrobus, & S. J. Ellman (Eds.), *The Mind in Sleep: Psychology and Psychophysiology* (pp. 393–415). Hillsdale, NJ: Lawrence Erlbaum.

Aserinsky, E., & Kleitman N. (1953). Regular occurring periods of eye motility and concurrent phenomena during sleep. *Science, 118*: 4.

Baireuther, R. F. (1995). Influence of alcohol on manifest dream content. *Sleep Research, 24A*.

Baldridge, B. J., Kramer, M., Whitman, R. M., & Ornstein, P. H. (1968). Smoking and dreams. *Psychophysiology, 4*(3): 372–373.

Baldridge, P. B. (1966). Physical concomitants of dreaming and the effect of stimulation on dreams. *Ohio State Medical Journal, 62*(12): 1273–1275.

Baldridge, P. B., Whitman, R. M., Kramer, M., Ornstein, P. H., & Lansky, L. (1965). The effect of external physical stimuli on dream content. Presentation to Association for the Psychophysiological Study of Sleep, Washington.

Banys, P. (2002). Group therapy for alcohol dependence within a phase model of recovery. In: D. W. Brook & H. I. Spitz (Eds.), *The Group Therapy of Substance Abuse* (pp. 59–77). New York: Haworth Medical Press.

Barbano, M. F., & Cador, M. (2007). Opioids for hedonic experience and dopamine to get ready for it. *Psychopharmacology, 191*: 497–506.

Bassareo, V., & Di Chiara, G. (1999). Differential responsiveness of dopamine transmission to food-stimuli in nucleus accumbens shell/core compartments. *Neuroscience, 89*: 637–641.

Batson, H. W. (1980). The effects of cigarette-withdrawal and a related verbal stimulus on REM sleep and dreaming. *Dissertation Abstract International, 41*(4-b): 149-b.

Beaman, H. A. (2002). Self reported dream experiences of alcohol and amphetamine dependent men and women during their initial 30 days of abstinence. Dissertation Abstract. Accessed 21 October 2002, at: www.phddissertations.com/display_abstract.asp?dissertation_id=63.

Bedi, G., Preston, K. L., Epstein, D. H., Heishman, S. J., Marrone, G. F., Shaham, Y., & De Wit, H. (2011). Incubation of cue-induced cigarette craving during abstinence in human smokers. *Biological Psychiatry, 69*: 708–711.

Beresford, T. B., Blow, F. C., Bower, K. J., & Maddahian, E. (1988). A comparison of self-reported symptoms and DSM-III-R criteria for cocaine withdrawal. *American Journal of Drug and Acohol Abuse, 14*(3): 347–356.

Berger, D. M. (1980). Couple's reactions to male infertility and donor insemination. *American Journal of Psychiatry, 137*(9): 1047–1049.

Berridge, K. C. (2001). Reward learning: reinforcement, incentives and expectations. In: D. L. Medin (Ed.), *Psychology of Learning and Motivation* (vol. 40, pp. 223–278). New York: Academic Press.

Berridge, K. C., & Robinson, T. E. (1995). The mind of an addicted brain: neural sensitization of wanting versus liking. *Current Directions in Psychological Science, 4*: 71–76.

Berridge, K. C., & Robinson, T. E. (1998). What is the role of dopamine in reward: hedonic impact, reward learning, or incentive salience? *Brain Research Reviews, 28*: 309–369.

Berridge, K. C., & Robinson, T. E. (2003). Addiction. *Annual Review of Psychology, 54*: 25–53.

Bischof, M., & Bassetti, C. (2004). Total dream loss: a distinct neuropsychological dysfunction after bilateral PCA stroke. *Annals of Neurology, 56*: 583–586.

Blackburn, J. R., Pfaus, J. G., & Phillips, A. G. (1992). Dopamine functions in appetitive and defensive behaviours. *Progress in Neurobiology, 39*: 247–279.

Bob, P., Jasova, D., Bizik, G., & Raboch, J. (2011). Epileptiform activity in alcohol dependent patients and possibilities of its indirect measurement. *PlOS One,* 26 apr: 10.1371/journal.pone.0018678.

Bokert, E. G. (1968). The effects of thirst and related verbal stimulus on dream reports. *Dissertation Abstracts, 28*: 4753b.

Brauer, L. H., Cramblett, M. J., Paxton, D. A., & Rose, J. E. (2001). Haloperidol reduces smoking of both nicotine-containing and denicotinized cigarettes. *Psychopharmacology, 159*: 31–37.

Braun, A. R., Balkin, T. J., Wesenten, N. J., Carson, R. E., Varga, M., Baldwin, P., Selbie, S., Belenky, G., & Herscovitch, P. (1997). Regional cerebral blood flow throughout the sleep–wake cycle—an (H2O)-O-15-PET study. *Brain, 120*: 1173–1197.

Breger, L. (1967). Function of dreams. *Journal of Abnormal Psychology, Monograph, 72*(5): 1–28.

Breger, L., Hunter, R. W., & Lane, I. (1971). The effect of stress on dreams. *Psychological Issues, 7*: 3.

Brotini, S., Piani, A., Dolso, P., & Gigli, G.L. (2005). Lesioni bilaterali del globo pallido con disturbo comportamentale, prevalente deficit mnestico e delle funzioni esecutive: caso clinico. Poster presentation, *XXXII Congresso Nazionale Limpe*. Palermo: Italy.

Brown, S. (1985). *Treating the Alcoholic: A Developmental Model of Recovery.* New York: Wiley Press.

Brugger, P. (2008). The phantom limb in dreams. *Consciousness and Cognition, 17*(4): 1272–1278.

Carroll, D., Lewis, S. A., & Oswald, J. (1969). Effect of barbiturates on dream content. *Nature, 223*: 865–866.

Cartwright R. (1996). Dreams and adaptation to divorce. In: D. Barrett (Ed.), *Trauma and Dreams* (pp. 179–185). Cambridge, MA: Harvard University Press.

Cartwright, R. (2010). *The Twenty-four Hour Mind: The Role of Sleep and Dreaming in our Emotional Lives.* New York: Oxford University Press.

Childress, A. R., Ehrman, R. N., Wang, Z., Li, Y., Sciortino, N., Hakun, J., Jens, W., Suh, J., Listerud, J., Marques, K., Franklin, T., Langleben, D., Detre, J., & O'Brien, C. P. (2008). Prelude to passion: limbic activation by "unseen" drug and sexual cues. *Plos One, 1506*: 1–7.

Childress, A. R., Mozley, P. D., McElgin, W., Fitzgerald, J., Reivich, M., & O'Brien, C. P. (1999). Limbic activation during cue-induced cocaine craving. *American Journal of Psychiatry, 156*: 11–18.

Choi, S. Y. (1973). Dreams as a prognostic factor in alcoholism. *American Journal of Psychiatry, 130*: 699–702.

Christensen, R. L. (2009). A multi-level analysis of attentional biases in abstinent and non-abstinent problem drinkers. Dissertation. Florida State University College of Arts and Sciences.

Christo, G., & Franey, C. (1996). Addicts' drug-related dreams: their frequency and relationship to six-month outcomes. *Substance Use & Misuse, 31*: 1–15.

Cohen, D. (1977). *Dreams, Visions and Drugs: A Search for Other Realities.* New York: New Viewpoints.

Colace, C. (1999a). I sogni nei tossicodipendenti in stato di astinenza: osservazioni su due casi clinici. Poster presentation. 4° Riunione della Società Italiana di Ricerca sul Sonno (S.I.R.S.), Isola d Elba, 4–6 giugno.

Colace, C. (1999b). Dreams in abstinent opiate drug addicts: a case report study. *Sleep, 22*(1): 175–176.

Colace, C. (2000a). Sognare nelle dipendenze patologiche: implicazioni per la psicoanalisi e la ricerca sul sogno. Poster presentation. 5° Riunione della Società Italiana di Ricerca sul Sonno (S.I.R.S.), Isola d Elba, 9–11 giugno.

Colace, C. (2000b). Dreams in abstinent heroin addicts: four case reports. *Sleep and Hypnosis, 2*: 160–163.

Colace, C. (2000c). I sogni s'uso di eroina nella terapia del tossicodipendente: osservazioni preliminari. *Prevenzione e Salute. La Rassegna Italiana sulle Tossicodipendenze, 27*: 8–16.

Colace, C. (2001a). Needs and dreaming processes: observations on dreams of abstinent heroin addicts. *Sleep, 24*: A185.

Colace, C. (2001b). Drug dreams. IV Congresso Nazionale della Società Italiana di Medicina delle Tossicodipendenze. Turin, 17–19 October. Abstract Book, p. 75.

Colace, C. (2002). Stati motivazionali e sognare: osservazioni su drug-dreams. Poster presentation. 7° Riunione della Società Italiana di Ricerca sul Sonno (S.I.R.S.), Padova, 13–14 September 2002.

Colace, C. (2004a). Dreaming in addiction. A study on the motivational bases of dreaming processes. *Neuro-psychoanalysis, 6*(2): 167–181.

Colace, C. (2004b). I drug dreams come strumento clinico e prognostico. *Prevenzione e Salute. La Rassegna Italiana sulle Tossicodipendenze, 37*: 53–62.

Colace, C. (2006). Drug dreams in cocaine addiction. *Alcohol & Drug Review, 25*(2): 177.

Colace, C. (2007). I correlati neuroanatomici e neurobiologici dei drug dreams. *Prevenzione e Salute. La Rassegna Italiana sulle Tossicodipendenze, 48*: 5–16.

Colace, C. (2009a). Drug dreams, drug craving e misura dell'attività del sistema limbico attraverso il Limbic System Checklist (LSCL-33): un studio pilota su un caso clinico. *Salute & Prevenzione. La Rassegna Italiana sulle Tossicodipendenze, 52*: 85–91.

Colace, C. (2009b). Gli studi sull'effetto della frustrazione dei bisogni primari sul sognare e la recente ricerca e teoria sui processi onirici. *Psycofenia, XII*(20): 49–72.

Colace, C. (2009c). The study of bizarreness in young children's dreams: a way to test the disguise-censorship model. Poster presentation. International Neuropsychoanalysis Congress, 26–29 June, Paris.

Colace, C. (2010a). *Children's Dreams: From Freud's Observations to Modern Dream Research.* London: Karnac.

Colace, C. (2010b). Drug dreams in mescaline and LSD addiction. *American Journal on Addictions, 19*(2): 192.

Colace, C. (2011). The nature of wish-fulfilment in young children's dreams: further observations. *Poster presentation,* 2011 International Congress of Neuropsychoanalysis, 24–26 giugno, Berlin.

Colace, C. (2012). Dream bizarreness and the controversy between the neurobiological approach and the disguise censorship model: the contribution of children's dreams. *Neuropsychoanalysis, 14*(2): 165–174.

Colace, C. (2013). Are wish-fulfilment dreams of children the royal road for looking at the functions of dreams? *Neuropsychoanalysis* (in press).

Colace, C. (n.d.a). Drug dream as a signal of drug craving persistence in time. Submitted.

Colace, C (n.d.b). I drug dreams come "segnale di allerta" di recrudescenza del drug craving: un caso clinico. Submitted.

Colace, C., & Tuci, B. (1996). Early children's dreams are not bizarre. *Sleep Research, 25*: 147.

Colace, C., Belsanti, S., & Antermite, A. (n.d.). Temporolimbic system irritability as neurobiological substrate of drug dreaming in heroin-addicted subjects. Submitted.

Colace, C., Claps, M. A., Antognoli, A., Sperandio, R., Sardi, D., & Benedetti, A. (2010). Limbic system activity and drug dreaming in drug-addicted subjects. *Neuro-psychoanalysis, 12*(2): 201–206.

Colace, C., Doricchi, F., Di Loreto E., & Violani, C. (1993). Developmental qualitative and quantitative aspects of bizarreness in dream reports of children. *Sleep Research, 22*: 57.

Colace, C., Lagrutta, A., Galli, A., Miscia, A., Di Vito, C., Sardi, D., & Antognoli, A. (n.d.). Drinking dreams among alcoholic patients. In preparation.

Crick, F., & Mitchison, G. (1983). The function of REM sleep. *Nature, 304*: 111–114.

Daglish, M. R. C., & Nutt, D. J. (2003). Brain imaging studies in human addicts. *European Neuropsychopharmacology, 13*(6): 453–458.

Damasio, A. R. (1994). *Descartes' Error: Emotion, Reason, and the Human Brain*. New York: Grosset/Putnam.

Damsma, G., Pfaus, J. G., Wenkstern, D., Phillips, A. G., & Fibiger, H. C. (1992). Sexual behavior increases dopamine transmission in the nucleus accumbens and striatum of male rats: comparison with novelty and locomotion. *Behavioral Neuroscience, 106*: 181–191.

Di Chiara, G. (1995). The role of dopamine in drug abuse viewed from the perspective of its role in motivation. *Drug and Alcohol Dependence, 38*: 95–137.

Di Chiara, G. (1996). Psicobiologia delle tossicodipendenze. In: G. Serpelloni, R. Pirastu, & O. Brignoli (Eds.), *Medicina delle Tossicodipendenze* (pp. 1–11). Florence: SEMG.

Di Chiara, G., & Imperato, A. (1988). Drugs abused by humans preferentially increase synaptic dopamine concentrations in mesolimbic system of freely moving rats. *Proceedings of the National Academy of Sciences, U.S.A., 85*: 5274–5278.

Di Chiara, G., Tanda, G., Bassareo, V., Pontieri, F., Acquas, E., Fenu, S., Cadoni, C., & Carboni, E. (1999). Drug addiction as a disorder of associative learning: role of nucleus accumbens shell/extended amygdala dopamine. *Annals of the New York Academy of Sciences, 29*: 461–485.

DeCicco, T. L., & Higgins, H. (2009). Dreams of recovering alcoholics: mood, dream content, discovery, and the storytelling method of dream interpretation. *International Journal of Dream Research, 2*: 45–51.

Denzin, N. K. (1988). Alcoholic dreams. *Alcoholism Treatment Quarterly, 5*: 133–139.

Dimauro, P. E. (1999). Le sostanze: aspetti clinico-farmacologici. In: P. E. Dimauro & V. Patussi (Eds.), *Dipendenze* (pp. 63–94). Rome: Carocci Editore.

Domhoff, G. W. (2001). Why did empirical dream researchers reject Freud? A critique of historical claims by Mark Solms. *Dreaming, 14*: 3–17.

Domhoff, G. W. (2005). Refocusing the neurocognitive approach to dreams: a critique of the Hobson versus Solms debate. *Dreaming, 15*: 3–20.

Falk, J. L., Dews, P. B., & Schuster, C. R. (1983). Commonalities in the environmental control of behavior. In: P. K. Levinson, D. R. Gerstein, & D. R. Maloff (Eds.), *Commonalities in Substance Abuse and Habitual Behavior* (pp. 47–110). Lexington, MA: Lexington Books.

Fibiger, H. C., & Phillips, A. G. (1987). Role of catecholamine transmitters in reward system: implications for the neurobiology of affect. In: J. Engel & L. Oreland (Eds.), *Brain Reward Systems and Abuse* (pp. 61–74). New York: Raven Press.

Fisher, C. (1970). Some psychoanalytic implications of recent research on sleep and dreaming. In: L. Madow & L. H. Snow (Eds.), *The Psychodynamic Implications of the Physiological Studies on Dreams* (pp. 152–167). Springfield, IL: Thomas.

Fisher, S., & Greenberg, R. P. (1977). *The Scientific Credibility of Freud's Theories and Therapy*. New York: Basic Books.

Fiss, H. (1979). Current dream research: a psychobiological perspective. In: B.B. Wolman (Ed), *Handbook of Dreams* (pp. 20–75). New York: Van Nostrand Reinhold.

Fiss, H. (1980). Dream content and response to withdrawal from alcohol. *Sleep Research, 9*: 152.

Fiss, H. (1991). Experimental strategies for the study of the function of dreaming. In: S. Ellman & J. Antrobus (Eds.), *The Mind in Sleep* (pp. 308–326). New York: Wiley.

Flowers, L. K., & Zweben, J. E. (1996). The dream interview method in addiction recovery: a treatment guide. *Journal of Substance Abuse Treatment, 13*: 99–105.

Flowers, L. K., & Zweben, J. E. (1998). The changing role of "using" dreams in addiction recovery. *Journal of Substance Abuse Treatment, 15*: 193–200.

Fosshage, J. L. (1997). The organizing functions of dream mentation. *Contemporary Psychoanalysis, 33*(3): 429–458.

Foulkes, D. (1985). *Dreaming: A Cognitive–Psychological Approach*. Hillsdale, NJ: Lawrence Erlbaum.

Franklin, T. R., & Druhan, J. P. (2000). Expression of Fos-related antigens in the nucleus accumbens and associated regions following exposure to a cocaine-paired environment. *European Journal of Neuroscience, 12*: 2097–2106.

Franklin, T. R., Lohoff, F. W., Wang, Z., Sciortino, N., Harper, D., Li, Y., Jens, W., Cruz, J., Kampman, K., Ehrman, R., Berrettini, W., Detre, J. A., O'Brien, C. P., & Childress, A. R. (2009). DAT genotype modulates brain and behavioral responses elicited by cigarette cues. *Neuropsychopharmacology, 34*: 717–728

Freud, S. (1900a). *The Interpretation of Dreams. S.E., 4–5*. London: Hogarth Press.

Freud, S. (1901a). On dreams. *S.E., 5*: 633–685. London: Hogarth Press.

Freud, S. (1905c). *Jokes and their Relation to the Unconscious. S.E., 8*. London: Hogarth Press.

Freud, S. (1910a). Five lectures on psycho-analysis. *S.E., 11*: 3–55. London: Hogarth Press.

Freud, S. (1915c). Instincts and their vicissitudes. *S.E., 14*: 109–140. London: Hogarth Press.

Freud, S. (1916–1917). *Introductory Lectures on Psycho-Analysis. S.E., 15–16.* London: Hogarth Press.

Freud, S. (1917d). A metapsychological supplement to the theory of dreams. *S.E., 14*: 222–235. London: Hogarth Press.

Freud, S. (1925d). An autobiographical study. *S.E., 20*: 3–70. London: Hogarth Press.

Freud, S. (1933a). *New Introductory Lectures on Psychoanalysis. S.E., 22.* London: Hogarth Press.

Gaillard, J. M., & Moneme, A. (1977). Modification of dream content after preferential blockade of mesolimbic and mesocortical dopaminergic systems. *Journal of Psychiatric Research, 13*(4): 247–256.

Garavan, H. (2010). Insula and drug cravings. *Brain Structure and Function, 214*(5–6): 593–601.

Gerevich, J., & Meggyes, K. (2004). Are dreams about drugs, substances, or treatment the royal road to prediction of treatment outcome? *Journal of Nervous and Mental Disease, 192*(10): 720.

Gillispie, C. (2010). Relapse dreams. A hidden message? *California Together, 4*(4): 1.

Goldstein, R. Z., & Volkow, N. D. (2002). Drug addiction and its underlying neurobiological basis: neuroimaging evidence for the involvement of the frontal cortex. *American Journal of Psychiatry, 159*(10): 1642–1652.

Goldstein, R. Z., Tomasi, D., Alia-Klein, N., Carrillo, J. H., Maloney, T., Woicik, P. A., Wang, R., Telang, F., & Volkow, N. D. (2009). Dopaminergic response to drug words in cocaine addiction. *Journal of Neuroscience, 29*(18): 6001–6006.

Gorelick, D. A., Kim, Y. K., Bencherif, B., Boyd, S. J., Nelson, R., Copersino, M., Endres, C. J., Dannals, R. F., & Frost, J. J. (2005). Imaging brain mu-opioid receptors in abstinent cocaine users: time course and relation to cocaine craving. *Biological Psychiatry., 15 57*(12): 1573–1582.

Greenberg, J., & Mitchell, S. A. (1983). Object relations in psychoanalytic theory. Cambridge, MA: Harvard University Press.

Grünbaum, A. (1984). *The Foundations of Psychoanalysis. A Philosophical Critique.* Los Angeles, CA: University of California Press.

Guénole, F., Marcaggi, G., & Baleyte, J. M. (2013). Do dreams really guard sleep? Evidence for and against Freud's theory of the basic function of dreaming. *Frontiers in Psychology, 4*(17): 1–3.

Gürpinar, D., & Tokuçoğlu, L. (2006). Bağimlilik Yapan maddeleri kullanmak için duyulan arzu ve bu maddelerle ilgili rüyalar. [Craving of addictive substances and the dreams related with these substances]. Bağimlilik Derğisi, *Journal of Depencence, 7*: 38–43.

Hall, C. S. (1966). A comparison of dreams of four groups of hospitalized mental patients with each other and with a normal population. *Journal of Nervous Mental Diseases, 143*: 135–139.

Hajek, P., & Belcher, M. (1991). Dream of absent-minded transgression: an empirical study of a cognitive withdrawal symptom. *Journal of Abnormal Psychology, 100*: 487–491.

Hartmann, E. (2011). *The Nature and the Functions of Dreaming*. New York: Oxford University Press.

Hartmann, E., Russ, D., Oldfield, M., Falke, R., & Skoff, B. (1980). Dream content: effects of L- DOPA. *Sleep Research, 9*: 153.

Hernandez, J. M. (1992). The subjective meaning of crack in black females. A phenomenological study based on dreams and early recollections during detoxification. Dissertation (no. 9303570). The Union Institute, Cincinnati, Ohio.

Herr, S. R., Montoya, I. D., & Preston, K. (1994). Drug-related dreams in cocaine-dependent patients seeking treatment. NIH/NIDA, National Institute on Drug Abuse. Research Monograph Series no. 141. Problems of Drug Dependence, 1993: *Proceedings of the 55th Annual Scientific Meeting The College on Problems of Drug Dependence, II*: 154.

Hobson, J. A. (1988). *The Dreaming Brain*. New York: Basic Books.

Hobson, J. A. (2000). The ghost of Sigmund Freud haunts Mark Solm's dream theory. *Behavioral and Brain Sciences, 23*: 951–952.

Hobson, J. A. (2002). *Dreaming: An Introduction to Science of Sleep*. New York: Oxford University Press.

Hobson, J. A. (2004). Freud returns? Like a bad dream. *Scientific American, 290*: 89.

Hobson, J. A. (2005). In bed with Mark Solms? What a nightmare! A reply to Domhoff (2005). *Dreaming, 15*: 21–29.

Hobson, J. A. (2006). Dream debate. Should Freud's dream theory be abandoned? Hobson (yes) vs Solms (no). Presented to the Conference "Toward a Science of Consciousness", Tucson, Arizona, April.

Hobson, J. A. (2009). REM sleep and dreaming: towards a theory of proto-consciousness. *Nature Reviews Neuroscience, 10*: 803–813.

Hobson, J. A. (2013). Ego Ergo Sum: toward a psychodinamic neurology. *Contemporary Psychoanalysis, 49*(2): 142–164.

Hobson, J. A., & Friston, K. J. (2012). Waking and dreaming consciousness: neurobiological and functional consideration. *Progress in Neurobiology, 98*(1): 82–98.

Hobson, J. A., Pace-Schott, E. F., & Stickgold, R. (2000). Dreaming and the brain: toward a cognitive neuroscience of conscious states. *Behavioral and Brain Sciences, 23*(6): 793–842.

Hoffmann, H. C. (2002). Communal individualism: managing conflict in Alcoholics Anonymous. PhD Dissertation. University of Georgia, Athens, Georgia.

Hutcheson, D. M., Everitt, B. J., Robbins, T. W., & Dickinson, A. (2001). The role of withdrawal in heroin addiction: enhances reward or promotes avoidance? *Nature Neuroscience, 4*: 943–947.

Ikemoto, S., & Panksepp, J. (1996). Dissociations between appetitive and consummatory responses by pharmacological manipulations of reward-relevant brain regions. *Behavioral Neuroscience, 110*: 331–345.

Ikemoto, S., & Panksepp, J. (1999). The role of nucleus accumbens dopamine in motivated behavior: unifying interpretation with special reference to reward-seeking. *Brain Research Reviews, 31*: 6–41.

Ivanets, N. N. & Vinnikova, M. A. (2001). Diagnostic criteria of the severity of the pathologic drive to narcotics. *Zh Nevrol Psikhiatr Im S S Korsacova, 101*(8): 4–7.

Jakobson, A. J., Fitzgerald, P. B., & Conduit, R. (2012). Induction of visual dream reports after transcranial direct current stimulation (tDCs) during Stage 2 sleep. *Journal of Sleep Research, 21*(4): 369–379.

Jasova, D., Bob, P., & Fedor-Freybergh, P. (2007). Alcohol craving, limbic irritability, and stress. *Medical Science Monitor, 13*(12): CR543–547.

Jerry, P. A. (1997). Psychodynamic psychotherapy of the intravenous cocaine abuser. *Journal of Substance Abuse Treatment, 14*: 319–322.

Johnson, B. (2001). Drug dreams: a neuropsychoanalytic hypothesis. *Journal of the American Psychoanalytic Association, 49*: 75–96.

Johnson, B. (2003a). Psychological addiction, physical addiction, addictive character, and addictive personality disorder: a nosology of addictive disorders. *Canadian Journal of Psychoanalysis, 11*: 135–160.

Johnson, B. (2003b). Commentary on "Understanding addictive vulnerability". *Neuropsychoanalysis, 5*(1): 29–34.

Johnson, B. (2008a). Just what lies "Beyond the pleasure principle". *Neuropsychoanalysis, 10*(2): 201–212.

Johnson, B. (2008b). Drugs of abuse, sleep and the quality of life. In: J. C. Verster, S. R. Pandi-Perumal, & D. L. Streiner (Eds.), *Sleep and Quality of Life in Medical Illness* (pp. 341-346). Totawa, NJ: Humana Press.

Johnson, B. (2011). Psychoanalytic treatment of psychological addiction to alcohol (alcohol abuse). *Frontiers in Psychology, 2*: article 362. doi: 10.3389/fpsyg.2011.00362.

Johnson, B. (2012). Drug abuse, dreams and nightmare. In: J. C. Verster, K. Brady, M. Galanter, & P. Conrod (Eds.), *Drug Abuse and Addiction in Medical Illness: Causes, Consequences and Treatment* (pp. 385–392) New York: Springer.

Johnson, R. A. (2000). Relationship of dreams of drinking and negative expectancies to alcohol treatment outcome in a veterans administration alcoholic inpatient treatment population. *Dissertation Abstract International. Section B: The Sciences & Engineering, 61*(6-B): 3280.

Jones, D. S., Krotick, S., Johnson, B., & Morrison, A. P. (2005). Clinical challenge: waiting for rescue, an attorney who will not advocate for himself. *Harvard Review of Psychiatry, 13*: 344–356.

Jorgensen, E. D., & Salwen, R. (2000). Treatment of dually diagnosed adolescents: the individual therapeutic alliance within a day treatment model. *National Institute on Drug Abuse Publication* No. 00–4151.

June, H. L., Foster, K. L., McKay, P. F., Carroll, M. R., Seyoum, R., Woods, J. E., Harvey, S. C., Eiler, W. J. A. II, Grey, C., McCane, S., Garcia, M., Jones, C. M., Mason, D., Cummings, R., Yin, W., Cook, J. M., & Skolnick, P. (2003). The reinforcing properties of alcohol are mediated by GABA(A1) receptors in the ventral pallidum. *Neuropsychopharmacology, 28*: 2124–2137.

Kaplan-Solms, K., & Solms, M. (2000). *Clinical Studies in Neuro-Psychonalysis*. Madison CT: International Universities Press.

Kassel, J. D., & Shiffman, S. (1992). What can hunger teach us about drug craving? A comparative analysis of the two constructs. *Advances in Behaviour Research and Therapy, 14*: 141–167.

Kay, D. C., Eisenstein, R. B., & Jasinski, D. R. (1969). Morphine effects on human REM state, waking state, and NREM sleep. *Psychopharmacology, 14*: 404–416

Kaufman, E. (Ed.) (1994). *Psychotherapy of Addicted Persons*. New York: Guilford Press.

Keeley, J. D. (2004). The process of recovery: dreams of women in midlife during midphase recovery from alcoholism. Dissertation. Alliant International University, Fresno, AAT 3135489.

Kelley, A. E., & Berridge, K. E. (2002). The neuroscience of natural rewards: relevance to addictive drugs. *Journal of Neuroscience, 22*: 3306–3311.

Kibira, C. (1994). The dreams of women in early recovery. Unpublished doctoral dissertation, California School of Professional Psychology, Berkeley/Alameda.

Klein, G. S. (1965). Peremptory ideation. Structure and force in motivated ideas. Presented to the Conference on Cognition and Clinical Psychology, University of Colorado, Boulder, Colorado, 20 April.

Kline, P. (1971). *Facts and Fantasy in Freudian Theory*. London: Methuen.

Koob, G. F. (2011). Neurobiology of addiction. *Focus, IX*(1): 55–65.

Koob, G. F., & Le Moal, M. (1997). Drug abuse: hedonic homeostatic dysregulation. *Science, 278*: 52–58.

Koob, G. F., & Le Moal, M. (2006). *Neurobiology of Addiction.* London: Academic Press.

Koob, G. F., & Volkow, N. (2010). Neurocircuitry of addiction. *Neuropsychopharmacology Reviews, 35*: 217–238.

Kramer, M. (2007). *The Dream Experience: A Systematic Exploration.* New York: Routledge.

Laplanche, J., & Pontalis, J.-B. (1973). *The Language of Psycho-Analysis.* New York: W. W. Norton.

Larimer, M. E., Palmer, R. S., & Marlatt, G. A. (1999). Relapse prevention. An overview of Marlatt's cognitive-behavioral model. *Alcohol Research & Health, 23*(2): 151–160.

LeDoux, J. (1996). *The Emotional Brain: The Mysterious Underpinnings of Emotional Life.* New York: Simon & Schuster.

Levin, R., & Nielsen T. A. (2007). Disturbed dreaming. Posttraumatic stress disorder, and affect distress: a review of a neurocognitive model. *Psychological Bulletin, 133*(3): 482–528.

Leyton, M., Boileau, I., Benkelfat, C., Diksic, M., Baker, G. B., & Dagher, A. (2002). Amphetamine-induced increases in extracellular dopamine, drug wanting, and novelty seeking: A PET/[11C]raclopride study in healthy men. *Neuropsychopharmacology, 27*: 1027–1035.

Leyton, M., Casey, K. F., Delaney, J. S., Kolivakis, T., & Benkelfat, C. (2005). Cocaine craving, euphoria, and self-administration: a preliminary study of the effect of catecholamine precursor depletion. *Behavioral Neuroscience, 119*: 1619–1627.

Lieberman, M. D., & Eisenberger, N. I. (2009). Pains and pleasures of social life. *Science, 323*: 890–891.

London, E. D., Ernst, M., Grant, G., Bonson, K., & Weinstein, A. (2000). Orbitofrontal cortex and human drug abuse: functional imaging. *Cerebral Cortex, 10*: 334–342.

Looney, M. (1972). The dreams of heroin addicts. *Social Work, 17*: 23–28.

Makaric, E. (1979). Importance of dreams of alcoholics in their treatment and abstinence. *Socijana Psihijatrija, 7*: 41–53.

Manna, V., & Ruggiero, S. (2001).Dipendenze patologiche da sostanze. Comorbilità psichiatrica o continuum psicopatologico? *Rivista di Psichiatria, 36*(1): 1–13.

Maquet, P., Peters, J. M., Aerts, J., Delfiore, G., Degueldre, C., Luxen, A., & Franck, G. (1996). Functional neuroanatomy of human rapid-eye movement sleep and dreaming. *Nature, 386*(6596): 163–166.

Maremmani, I., Canoniero, S., & Pacini, M. (2002). Psico(pato)logia dell' "addiction". Un'ipotesi interpretativa. *Annali dell'Istituto superiore di sanità, 38*(3): 241–257.

Maremmani, I., Canoniero, S., & Zolesi, O. (1999). Forme cliniche del craving e farmaci anticraving. *Itaca, 7*: 20–40.

Marshall, S. (1995). *Your Dream of Recovery: Dream Interpretation and the 12 Steps*. Virginia Beach, VA: ARE Press.

Massetani, R., Lucchetti, R., Piccini, P., & Bianchi, F. (1986). Dream recall and dream content in levodopa-treated Parkinsonian patients. *Research Communications in Psychology, Psychiatry & Behavior, 11*(2–3), 65–73.

Matsumoto K., Sera, M., Yonezawa, H., Takao, H., Fujiwara, S., & Shingai, N. (1998). Drinking dreams and continued abstinence: a study on alcoholics. *Japanese Journal of Addiction & Family, 15*(4): 427–433.

McCarley, R. W., & Hobson, J. A. (1977). The neurobiological origins of psychoanalytic dream theory. *American Journal of Psychiatry, 134*: 1211–1221.

McEwing, W. (1991). Dreams and recovery. *Dream Network Journal, 10*(4).

Meil, W. M., & See, R. E. (1997). Lesions of the basolateral amygdala abolish the ability of drug associated cues to reinstate responding during withdrawal from self-administered cocaine. *Behavioral Brain Research, 87*: 139–148.

Melis, M. R., & Argiolas, A. (1995). Dopamine and sexual behaviour. *Neuroscience and Biobehavioral Reviews, 19*: 19–38.

Meyers, A. (1988). *Cocaine: A Treatment Guide for Counselors*. Tucson, AZ. Research Associates.

Miller, J. M., Vorel, S. R., Tranguch, A. J., Kenny, E. T., Mazzoni, P., Van Gorp, W. G., & Kleber, H. D. (2006). Anhedonia after a selective bilateral lesion of the globus pallidus. *American Journal of Psychiatry, 163*(5): 786–788.

Miller, N. S., & Gold, M. S. (1994). Dissociation of "conscious desire" (craving) from and relapse in alcohol and cocaine dependence. *Annals of Clinical Psychiatry, 6*: 99–106.

Money, J. (1960). Phantom orgasm in the dreams of paraplegic men and women. *Archives of General Psychiatry, 3*: 373–382.

Mooney, A. J., Eisenberg, A., & Eisenberg, H. (1992). *The Recovery Book*. New York: Workman.

Moore, R. A. (1962). The manifest dream of alcoholism. *Quarterly Journal of Studies on Alcohol, 23*: 583–589.

Morrison, R. A. (1990). Dream mapping in chemical dependency. *Alcohol Treatment Quarterly, 7*(3): 113–120.

Moscovitz, C., Moses, H., & Klawans, H. L. (1978). Levodopa-induced psychosis: a kindling phenomenon. *American Journal of Psychiatry*, 135(6): 669–675.

Mulder, T. H., Hochstenbach, J, Dijkstra, P. U., & Geertzen, J. H. (2008). Born to adapt, but not in your dreams. *Consciousness and Cognition*, 17(4): 1266–1271.

Muzio, J. N., Roffwarg, H. P., & Kaufman, E. (1966). Alterations in the nocturnal sleep cycle resulting from LSD. *Electroenceph Clinical Neurophysiology*, 21: 313–324.

Nader, K., & van der Kooy, D. (1994). The motivation produced by morphine and food is isomorphic: approaches to specific motivational stimuli are learned. *Psychobiology*, 22: 68–76.

Naqvi, N. H., & Bechara, A. (2009). The hidden island of addiction: the insula. *Trends in Neurosciences*, 32(1): 56–67.

Naqvi, N. H., Rudrauf, D., Damasio, H., & Bechara, A. (2007). Damage to the insula disrupts addiction to cigarette smoking. *Science*, 315: 531–534.

Nausieda, P., Weiner, W., Kaplan, L., Weber, S., & Klawans, H. (1982). Sleep disruption in the course of chronic levodopa therapy: an early feature of the levodopa psychosis. *Clinical Neuropharmacology*, 5: 183–194.

Nestler, E. J. (2001). Molecular basis of long-term plasticity underlying addiction. *Nat. Rev. Neuroscience*, 2: 119–128.

Nestler, E. J. (2005). Is there a common molecular pathway for addiction? *Nature Neuroscience*, 8(11): 1445–1449.

Newton, P. (1970). Recalled dream content and the maintenance of body image. *Journal of Abnormal Psychology*, 76: 134–139.

Niaura, R. S., Rohsenow, D. J., Binkoff, J.A., Monti, P. M., Pedraza, M., & Abrams, D. B. (1998). Relevance of cue reactivity to understanding alcohol and smoking relapse. *Journal of Abnormal Psychology*, 97: 133–152.

Nielsen, T. A., & Levin, R. (2007). Nightmares: a new neurocognitive model. *Sleep Medicine Reviews*, 11: 295–310.

Nigro, G., & Bergesio C. (2011). Delayed hypoxic leukoencephalopathy in a substance abuse patient: a case report. *Internet Journal of Psychiatry*, 1(1): DOI: 10.5580/1412.

Nofzinger, E., Mintun, M., Wiseman, M., Kupfer, D., & Moore, R. (1997). Forebrain activation in REM sleep: an FDG PET study. *Brain Research*, 770: 192–201.

Oswald, I. (1969). Human brain protein, drugs and dreams. *Nature*, 223: 893–897.

Oudiette, D., Dealberto, M. J., Uguccioni, G., Golmard, J. L., Merino-Andreu, M., Tafti, M., Garma, L., Schwartz, S., & Arnulf, I. (2012). Dreaming without REM sleep. *Consciousness and Cognition, 21*(3): 1129–1140.

Panksepp, J. (1998). *Affective Neuroscience: The Foundations of Human and Animal Emotions.* Oxford: Oxford University Press.

Parker, J. (1999). Dream in addiction treatment. *Electric Dreams, 6*(5). Retrieved July 11, 2000 from Electric Dreams on the World Wide Web: www.dreamgate.com/electric-dreams.

Parker, J., & Alford, C. (2009). The dreams of male and female abstinent alcoholics in stage II recovery compared to non alcoholic controls: are the differences significant? *International Journal of Dream Research, 2*(2): 73–84.

Pavlick, M., Hoffman, E., & Rosenberg, H. (2009). A nationwide survey of American alcohol and drug craving assessment and treatment practices. *Addiction Research and Theory, 17*(6): 591–600.

Perogamvros, L., & Schwartz, S. (2012). The roles of the reward system in sleep and dreaming. *Neuroscience and Biobehavioral Reviews, 36*: 1934–1951.

Persico, A. M. (1992). Predictors of smoking cessation in a sample of Italian smokers. *International Journal of the Addictions, 27*(6): 683–695.

Peters, K. A. (2000). The dreams of alcoholic men in early sobriety. Dream Time Articles. Association for the Study of Dreams. Accessed 16 May 2001 at: www.asdrems.org/magazine/articles/peters_recovery.htm

Peterson, N. D. J., Henke, P. G., & Hayes, Z. (2002). Limbic system function and dream content in university students. *Journal of Neuropsychiatry and Neurosciences, 14*: 283–288.

Petrakis, I. L., Trevisan, L., D'Souza, C., Gil, R., Krasnicki, S., Webb, E., Heninger, G., Cooney, N., & Krystal, J. H. (1999). CSF monoamine metabolite and beta endorphin levels in recently detoxified alcoholics and healthy controls: prediction of alcohol cue-induced craving? *Alcohol Clinical Experimental Research, 23*(8): 1336–1341.

Pickens, C. L., Airavaara, M., Theberge, F., Fanous, S., Hope, B. T., & Shaham, Y. (2011). Neurobiology of the incubation of drug craving. *Trends in Neurosciences, 34*(8): 411–420.

Piomelli, D. (2001). Cannabinoid activity curtails cocaine craving. *Nature Medicine, 7*(10): 1099–1100.

Pivik, R. T., Zarcone, V., Dement, W. C., & Hollister, L. E. (1972). Delta-9-tetrahydrocannabinol and synhexl: effects on human sleep patterns. *Clinical Pharmacological Therapy, 13*: 426–435.

Pontieri, F. E., Tanda, G., & Di Chiara, D. (1995). Intravenous cocaine, morphine and amphetamine preferentially increase extracellular dopamine in the "shell" as compared with the "core" of the rat nucleus accumbens. *Proceedings of the National Academy of Sciences, U.S.A., 92*: 12304–12308.

Popper, K. (1959). *The Logic of Scientific Discovery*. London: Hutchinson.

Popper, K. (1963). *Conjectures and Refutations. The Growth of Scientific Knowledge*. London: Routledge.

Pulvirenti, L., & Koob, G. F. (1990). Role of the nucleus accumbens in drug dependence: implications for affective disorder. In: G. L. Gessa & G. Serra (Eds.), *Dopamine and Mental Depression* (pp. 39–49). Oxford: Pergamon Press.

Ramsey, G. W. (1953). Studies in dreaming. *Psychology Bulletin, 50*: 432–455.

Rawson, R. A., Obert, J. L., McCann, M. J, & Ling, W. (1993). Neurobehavioral treatment for cocaine dependency: a preliminary evaluation. In: F. M. Tims & C. G. Leukefeld (Eds.), *Cocaine Treatment: Research and Clinical Perspective*. NIDA Research Monograph 135. Rockville, MD.

Reed, H. (1984). From alcoholic to dream. *Voices, 20*: 62–69.

Reid, S. D., & Simeon, D. T. (2001). Progression of dreams of crack cocaine as a predictor of treatment outcome: a preliminary report. *Journal of Nervous and Mental Disease, 189*: 854–857.

Revonsuo, A. (2000). The interpretation of dreams: an evolutionary hypothesis of the functions of dreaming. *Behavioral and Brain Sciences, 23*(6): 877–901.

Roberts, R. J., Gorman, L. L., Lee, G. P., Hines, M. E., Richardson, E. D., Riggle, T. A., & Varney, N. R. (1992). The phenomenology of multiple partial seizure-like symptoms without stereotyped spells: an epilepsy spectrum disorder? *Epilepsy Research, 13*: 167–177.

Robinson, T. E., & Berridge, K. C. (1993). The neural basis of drug craving: an incentive-sensitization theory of addiction. *Brain Research Reviews, 18*: 247–291.

Robledo, P., & Koob, G. F. (1993). Two discrete nucleus accumbens projection areas differentially mediate cocaine self-administration in the rat. *Behavioral Brain, 55*: 159–166.

Romo, R., & Schultz, W. (1990). Dopamine neurons of the monkey midbrain: contingencies of responses to active touch during self-initiated arm movements. *Journal of Neurophysiology, 63*: 592–606.

Ryan, J. (1961). Dreams of paraplegics. *Archives of General Psychiatry, 5*: 286–291.

Sacks, O. (1985). *The Man Who Mistook His Wife for a Hat*. London: Duckworth.

Sacks, O. (1990). *Awakenings*. New York: Harper Collins.

Schredl, M. (1999). Dream recall in patients with primary alcoholism after acute withdrawal. *Sleep and Hypnosis*, 1(1): 35–40.

Scott, E. M. (1968). Dreams of alcoholics. *Perceptual and Motor Skills, 26*: 1315–1318.

Seligman, M., & Yellen, A. (1987). What is a dreaming? *Behaviour Research and Therapy*, 25(1): 1–24.

Sell, L. A., Morris, J., Bearn, J., Frackowiak, R. S., Friston, K. J., & Dolan, R. J. (1999). Activation of reward circuitry in human opiate addicts. *European Journal of Neuroscience, 11*: 1042–1048.

Shalev, U., Morales, M., Hope, B., Yap, J., & Shaham, Y. (2001). Time-dependent changes in extinction behavior and stress-induced reinstatement of drug-seeking following withdrawal from heroin in rats. *Psychopharmacology, 156*: 98–107.

Sharpe, D. (1985). Memories of a smoker. *Nursing Times*, November, p. 41.

Shevrin, H. (1997). Psychoanalysis as the patient: high in feeling, low in energy. *Journal of the American Psychoanalytic Association, 45*: 841–864.

Shevrin, H. (2001). Drug dreams: an introduction. *Journal of the American Psychoanalytic Association, 49*: 69–73.

Shukla, G. D., Sahu, S. C., Tripathi, R. P., & Gupta, D. K. (1982). Phantom limb: a phenomenological study. *British Journal of Psychiatry, 141*: 54–58.

Smaldino, A. (1991). Substance abuse nightmares and the combat veteran with PTSD: a focus on the mourning process. In: A. Smaldino (Ed.), *Psychoanalytic Approaches to Addiction* (pp. 28–50). New York: Brunner/Mazel.

Smith, K. S., Tindell, A. J., Aldridge, J. W., & Berridge, K. C. (2009). Ventral pallidum roles in reward and motivation. *Behavioral Brain Research, 196*(2): 155–167.

Smith, M. R., Antrobus, J. S., Gordon, E., Tucker, M. A., Hirota, Y., Wamsley, E. J., Ross, L., Doan, T., Chaklader A., & Emery, R. N. (2004). Motivation and affect in REM sleep and the mentation reporting process. *Consciousnessand Cognition, 13*: 501–511.

Solms, M. (1995). New findings on the neurological organization of dreaming: implications for psychoanalysis. *Psychoanalytic Quarterly, 64*: 43–67.

Solms, M. (1997). *The Neuropsychology of Dreams: A Clinico-Anatomical Study*. Mahwah, NJ: Lawrence Erlbaum.

Solms, M. (1999). Dreams. Accessed March 2001 at: (www.abc.net. au/rn/talks/8.30/helthrpt/stories/s44369.htm).

Solms, M. (2000). Dreaming and REM sleep are controlled by different brain mechanisms. *Behavioral and Brain Sciences, 23*: 843–850.

Solms, M. (2004). Freud returns. *Scientific American, 290*: 83–88.

Solms, M. (2006). Dream debate. Should Freud's dream theory be abandoned? Hobson (yes) vs Solms (no). Presented to the Conference "Toward a Science of Consciousness", held in April at Tucson, Arizona.

Solms, M. (2011). Neurobiology and the neurological basis of dreaming. In: P. Montagna & S. Chokroverty (Eds.), *Handbook of Clinical Neurology*, 98 (3rd series) Sleep Disorders—Part 1 (pp. 519–544). New York: Elsevier.

Solms, M., & Turnbull, O. (2002). *The Brain and the Inner World: An Introduction to the Neuroscience of Subjective Experience*. New York: Other Press.

Solms, M., & Turnbull, O. (2011). What is neuropsychoanalysis? *Neuropsychoanalysis, 13*(2): 133–145.

Steinig, J., Foraita, R., Happe, S., & Heinze, M. (2011). Perception of sleep and dreams in alcohol-dependent patients during detoxication and abstinence. *Alcohol and Alcoholism, 46*(2): 143–147.

Stewart, C. (1999). Investigation of cigarette smokers who quit without treatment. *Journal of Drug Issues, 29*(1): 167–185.

Stinus, L., Le Moal, M., & Koob, G. F. (1990). Nucleus accumbens and amygdala are possible substrates for the aversive stimulus effects of opiate withdrawal. *Neuroscience, 37*: 767–773.

Světlák, M., Bob, P., & Kukleta, M. (2010). Complex partial seizure-like symptoms and smoking in university students. *Scripta Medica, 83*(2): 124–129.

Tart, C. T. (1969). The "high" dream: a new state of consciousness. In: C. T. Tart (Ed.), *Altered States of Consciousness* (pp. 169–174). New York: John Wiley.

Teicher, M. H., Glod, C. A., Surrey, J., & Swett, C. (1993). Early childhood abuse and limbic system ratings in adult psychiatric outpatients. *Journal of Neuropsychiatry and Clinical Neuroscience, 5*: 301–306.

Tindell, A. J., Berridge, K. C., & Aldridge, J. W. (2004). Ventral pallidal representation of Pavlovian cues and reward: population and rate codes. *Journal of Neuroscience, 24*: 1058–1069.

Tobler, P. N., Fiorillo C. D., & Schultz, W. (2005). Adaptive coding of reward value by dopamine neurons. *Science, 307*: 1642–1645.

Tracy, J. I. (1994). Assessing the relationship between craving and relapse. *Drug Alcohol Review, 13*: 71–77.

Valli, K. (2008). Threat simulation – the function of dreaming? Turun Yliopiston Julkaisujaannales Universitatis Turkuensis, Turku, Finland.

Van der Helm, E., & Walker, M. P. (2009). Overnight therapy? The role of sleep in emotional brain processing. *Psychology Bulletin, 135*(5): 731–748. (The numbers of the pages cited refer to the HTML version: www.ncbi.nlm.nih.gov/pmc/articles/PMC2890316/.)

Van der Helm, E., Yao, J., Dutt, S., Rao, V., Saletin, J. M., & Walker, M. P. (2011). REM sleep depotentiates amygdala activity to previous emotional experiences. *Current Biology, 21*(23): 2029–2032.

Vijayaraghavan, L., Vaidya, J. G., Humphreys, C. T., Beglinger, L. J., & Paradiso, S. (2008). Emotional and motivational changes after bilateral lesions of the globus pallidus. *Neuropsychology, 22*(3): 412–418

Vogel, G. W. (2000). Critique of current dream theories. *Behavioral and Brain Sciences, 23*: 1014–1016.

Volkow, N. D., Fowler, J. S., Wang, G. J., & Swanson, J. M. (2004). Dopamine in drug abuse and addiction: results from imaging studies and treatment implications. *Molecular Psychiatry, 9*: 557–569

Volkow, N. D., Wang, G. J., Telang, F., Fowler, J. S., Logan, J., Childress, A. R., Jayne, M., Yeming, M., & Wong, C. (2006). Cocaine cues and dopamine in dorsal striatum: mechanism of craving in cocaine addiction. *Journal of Neuroscience, 26*(24): 6583–6588.

Washton, A. M. (1989). Cocaine abuse. *Annals of Internal Medicine, 119*: 226–235.

Waterhouse, K. (1984). Where there's no smoke. *Daily Mirror,* 22 October, p. 10.

Weinberg, A. N. (1996). Mood changes, sleep patterns, and implications for treatment during withdrawal from cocaine: an application of opponent-process theory. Temple University, Dissertation No. 9707019m, Pennsylvania. Copyright UMI—Dissertations Publishing.

Whitman, R. M., Pierce, C. M., & Maas, J. (1960). Drug and dreams. In: L. Uhr & J. G. Miller (Eds.), *Drug and Behavior* (pp. 591–595). New York: John Wiley.

Whitman, R. M., Pierce, C. M., Maas, J. W., & Baldridge, B. (1961). Drug and dreams II: imipramine and prochlorperazine. *Comprehensive Psychiatry, 2*: 219–226.

Wise, R. A. (1989). The brain and reward in the neuropharmacological basis of reward. In: J. M Liebman & S. J. Cooper (Eds.), *The Neuropharmacological Basis of Reward* (pp. 377–424). Oxford: Oxford University Press.

Wise, R. A., & Bozarth, M. A. (1987). A psychomotor stimulant theory of addiction. *Psychological Review, 94*: 469–492.

Wolf, M. E. (2002). Addiction: making the connection between behavioral changes and neuronal plasticity in specific pathways. *Molecular Interventions, 2*: 146–157.

Wong, D. F., Kuwabara, H., Schretlen, D. J., Bonson, K. R., Zhou, Y., Ayon Nandi, J. R. B., Kimes, A. S., Maris, M. A., Kumar, A., Contoreggi, C., Links, J., Ernst, M., Rousset, O., Zukin, S., Grace, A. A., Rohde, C., Jasinski, D. R., & Gjedde, E. D. A. (2006). Increased occupancy of dopamine receptors in human striatum during cue-elicited cocaine craving. *Neuropsychopharmacology, 31*(12): 2716–2727.

Wood, P. (1968). Dreaming and social isolation. Unpublished PhD thesis, University of North Carolina. In: Webb W. B. (Ed.), *Sleep: an Experimental Approach*. London: Macmillan.

Wright, J., & Panksepp, J. (2012). An evolutionary framework to understand foraging, wanting, and desire: the neuropsychology of the seeking system *Neuropsychoanalysis, 14*(1): 5–39.

Wurmser, L. (1984). The role of superego conficts in substance abuse and their treatment. *International Journal of Psychoanalytic Psychotherapy, 10*: 227–258.

Yee, T., Perantie, D. C., Dhanani, N., & Brown, E. S. (2004a). Drug dreams in outpatients with bipolar disorder and cocaine dependence. *Journal of Nervous and Mental Disease, 192*(3): 238–242.

Yee, T., Perantie, D. C., Dhanani, N., & Brown, E. S. (2004b). Are dreams about drugs, substances, or treatment the royal road to prediction of treatment outcome? Reply to Gerevich and Meggyes. *Journal of Nervous and Mental Disease, 192*(10): 720.

Yoo, S. S., Gujar, N., Hu, P., Jolesz, F. A., & Walker, M. P. (2007). The human emotional brain without sleep—a prefrontal amygdala disconnect. *Current Biology, 17*(20): R877–878.

Young, A. M., & Herling, S. (1986). Drugs as reinforcers. In: S. R. Goldberg & I. P. Stolerman (Eds.), *Behavioral Analysis of Drug Dependence* (pp. 9–67). Orlando, FL: Academic Press,

Yu, C. K.-C., (2007). Cessation of dreaming and ventromesial frontal-region infarcts. *Neuro-Psychoanalysis, 9*: 83–90.

Ziegler, P. P. (2005). Addiction and the treatment of pain. *Substance Use & Misuse, 40*: 1945–1954.

INDEX

AA.VV., 75
Abrams, D. B., 26
Acquas, E., 29
Addolorato, G., 37
Aerts, J., 71, 77, 94
affective, 78
  brain reactivity, 79
  experience, 80, 82
  neuroethological perspective, 31
  neuroscience, xii, 30–31, 94, 108
  re-establishment, 79–80
  response, 26
  state, 79–80, 108
Agabio, R., 37
Airavaara, M., 41
Alcaro, A., 31, 98
alcoholic(s), 5, 20, 26, 31, 36–37, 40,
    53, 55, 61–62, 85, 103
  abstinent, 36, 85
  deprivation, 85
  dreams, 5, 50, 62, 66
  non-, 5
  patients, 5, 13, 32, 36–37, 50, 53,
    62–63, 98–99

recovering, 50
women, 50
Alcoholics Anonymous World
    Services, 6, 12, 40, 43, 62–63
Aldridge, J. W., 28
Alford, C., 3, 7, 11, 64
Alia-Klein, N., 29, 100
Ameisen, O., 7, 37
American Psychiatric Association,
    xi
amygdala, 26–27, 29, 97–98
  activity, 79
  basolateral, 31
  circuit, 79
  extended, 27, 31
Andersen, R. S., 74
Anderson, C. M., 98–99
Antermite, A., xiv, 7–10, 12–14, 18,
    22, 34–35, 41, 98–99, 101
Antognoli, A., xiv, 3, 7–8, 10–13,
    34–36, 98–101
Antrobus, J. S., 71–73, 100
anxiety, 15, 21, 49, 51, 53, 86, 109
Aragona, B. J., 76

Araujo, R. B., 7, 11, 30–31, 47–48, 50, 53
Argiolas, A., 76
Arkin, A. M., 5, 72–73
Arnulf, I., 94–95
Aserinsky, E., 5
Ayon Nandi, J. R. B., 100

Baireuther, R. F., 6
Baker, G. B., 29
Baldridge, B. J., 5–6, 40
Baldridge, P. B., 72
Baldwin, P., 71, 77, 94
Baleyte, J. M., 89–90
Balkin, T. J., 71, 77, 94
Banys, P., 7, 47
Barbano, M. F., 29
Bassareo, V., 29, 77
Bassetti, C., 94–95
Batson, H. W., 6, 40, 53–54
Beaman, H. A., 4, 7, 12, 14, 61
Bearn, J., 27
Bechara, A., 29
Bedi, G., 41
Beglinger, L. J., 29
behaviour(al), 30–31, 50, 73, 98
    functions, 31
    goal-seeking, 30, 82, 94
    high-risk, 27
    motivated, 73, 76
    repertoire, 79
    risky, 27
Belcher, M., xi–xii, 6, 8–9, 11–12, 14,
    16, 18, 34, 39, 42–43, 50, 54–55,
    62–63, 101
Belenky, G., 71, 77, 94
Belsanti, S., xiv, 7–10, 12–14, 18, 22,
    34–35, 41, 98–99, 101
Bencherif, B., 100
Benedetti, A., xiv, 3, 7–8, 10–13,
    34–35, 98–101
Benkelfat, C., 29
Beresford, T. B., 6, 47
Berger, D. M., 74
Bergesio, C., 29
Bernardi, M., 37
Berrettini, W., 26

Berridge, K. C., 25–26, 28–30, 82, 94,
    97, 100
Berridge, K. E., 76
Bianchi, F., 96
Binkoff, J. A., 26
Bischof, M., 94–95
Bizik, G., 98
Blackburn, J. R., 29, 76–77
Blow, F. C., 6, 47
Bob, P., 98–99
Boileau, I., 29
Bokert, E. G., 54, 72, 74, 90
Bonson, K. R., 27, 100
Bower, K. J., 6, 47
Boyd, S. J., 100
Bozarth, M. A., 28
Brauer, L. H., 29
Braun, A. R., 71, 77, 94
Breger, L., 54, 78–79
Brotini, S., 29
Brown, E. S., xi, 6, 8–9, 12–14, 19, 32,
    41, 43, 55, 63–64
Brown, S., 3, 10, 18, 20, 48, 66
Brugger, P., 78

Cadoni, C., 29
Cador, M., 29
Canoniero, S., 26, 32, 41
Capristo, E., 37
Caputo, F., 37
Carboni, E., 29
Carrillo, J. H., 29, 100
Carroll, D., 5
Carroll, M. R., 28
Carson, R. E., 71, 77, 94
Cartwright, R., xiii, 54, 78–79
Casey, K. F., 29
Chaklader, A., 71, 100
Childress, A. R., 26–27, 29, 100
Choi, S. Y., xi–xii, 3, 5–6, 13, 18, 31,
    36–37, 39–40, 53–54, 62–64, 81,
    85, 101
Christensen, R. L., 7, 9, 32
Christo, G., xi–xii, 3, 6–7, 9, 11–13, 18,
    31, 39–40, 42, 48, 55, 61, 63–64,
    101

Claps, M. A., xiv, 3, 7–8, 10–13,
        34–35, 98–101
Cohen, D., 5
Colace, C., xi–xiv, 3, 6–16, 18, 22,
        32–36, 39–41, 43, 48, 51–52, 54,
        64–66, 71–73, 77, 79–81, 85–86,
        88–90, 98–101
Colombo, G., 37
Conduit, R., 94–95
conscious(ness), 26 *see also*:
        unconscious(ness)
    anxiety, 53
    aspects, 27
    attitude, 53
    awareness, 26
    craving, 32
    desire, 26–27, 30, 48, 85, 87
    experience, 82
    feeling, 29
    functioning, 77
    perception, 52
    pre-, 53, 85
    proto-, 77
    sub-, 48
    urges, 29
Contoreggi, C., 100
Cook, J. M., 28
Cooney, N., 26
Copersino, M., 100
Cramblett, M. J., 29
craving, 4, 22, 26–27, 31, 34, 36–37, 41,
        43–44, 50, 59, 64, 86, 109 *see also*:
        conscious(ness),
        unconscious(ness)
    acute, 72
    alcohol, 4, 7, 32, 37, 50, 53, 57, 98
    anti-, 35, 48–49, 59, 104
    appetitive, 26, 34–35
    awareness of, 57
    cue-induced, 41
    daily, 41
    drug, xi–xv, 4, 8–9, 21–22, 25–37,
        40–41, 43–44, 47–59, 62–65,
        72–73, 76–83, 85, 87–88,
        97–106, 108–109
    frustration, 78, 81

    gratification, 66
    high, 31, 66
    increase of, 41, 62, 65
    incubation, 41
    intensity, 41, 49, 56, 82, 101
    low, 31, 66
    persistent, 29
    phobic, 26, 34–35
    powerful, 43, 48
    pressure, 78–79, 105
    reappearance of, 35
    satisfaction, 101, 105
    stimulation, 79
Crick, F., xiii, 77
Cruz, J., 26
Cummings, R., 28
Curtis, J. T., 76

Dagher, A., 29
Daglish, M. R. C., 27
Damasio, A. R., 31
Damasio, H., 29
Damsma, G., 77
Dannals, R. F., 100
Dealberto, M. J., 94–95
DeCicco, T. L., 7, 47, 64
Degueldre, C., 71, 77, 94
Delaney, J. S., 29
Delfiore, G., 71, 77, 94
Dement, W. C., 5
Denzin, N. K., xii, 5–6, 18, 40, 43, 53, 81
dependence, 104
    alcohol, 47, 61
    cocaine, 40
    drug, xii, xiv, 4, 9, 14, 25, 27, 30, 35,
        57, 99
    heroin, 51
    patient, 65
    polydrugs, 86
    substance, 4
Detre, J. A., 26
Detwiler, J. M., 76
De Wit, H., 41
Dews, P. B., 77
Dhanani, N., xi, 6, 8–9, 12–14, 19, 32,
        41, 43, 55, 63–64

Di Chiara, D., 27, 29, 32, 41, 77, 101
Dickinson, A., 25
Dijkstra, P. U., 75
Diksic, M., 29
Di Loreto, E., xiii
Dimauro, P. E., 32, 41
Di Vito, C., xiv, 10, 13, 36
Doan, T., 71, 100
Dolan, R. J., 27
Dolso, P., 29
Domenicali, M., 37
Domhoff, G. W., 90
Doricchi, F., xiii
dream(s) (*passim*) *see also*: alcoholic(s), sexual
  bizarreness, xiv, 95
  debate, xiii
  drinking, 11, 13, 31–32, 34, 36–37, 40, 48, 50, 53–55, 62, 66
  drive-related, 10, 75–77
  food, 10
  function of, 8, 58, 78–80, 105
  generation, 10
  gratifying, 54, 74
  interviewing, 8
  model, xii, xv
  motivational trigger, xii, 10
  process, xii–xiii
  psychology of, 8
  refusal, 21, 50
  relapse, 3, 18, 20, 66
  research, xii, xiv, 5, 8, 10
  satisfaction, 74, 88
  scenario, 14
  scene, 13
  smoking, 14, 62
  sobriety affirmation, 20, 66
  study of, 106
  theory, xii–xiv, 5, 8, 10, 81
  threat-related, 100
  wish-fulfilment, 79–80, 82
drug(s) (*passim*) *see also*: craving, dependence
  abuse, xiii, 20, 32, 43, 57, 66, 98–99, 104

cocaine, xiv, 4, 6–8, 11–12, 14, 16, 18, 20, 26, 36, 40–43, 52, 55–56, 62–64, 99, 103
heroin, xiii–xiv, 4–7, 9, 11–12, 14–17, 20–22, 36, 39–42, 51–52, 54, 56, 65–66, 85, 98–99, 103
LSD, xiv, 5–7, 11, 16, 86
methadone, 9, 11, 33–35, 51, 56
Druhan, J. P., 9
D'Souza, C., 26
Dutt, S., 79

Ehrman, R. N., 26
Eiler, W. J. A. II, 28
Eisenberg, A., 6, 10, 12, 40, 43, 55, 63
Eisenberg, H., 6, 10, 12, 40, 43, 55, 63
Eisenberger, N. I., 76
Eisenstein, R. B., 5
Emery, R. N., 71, 100
Endres, C. J., 100
Epstein, D. H., 41
Ernst, M., 27, 100
Everitt, B. J., 25

Falk, J. L., 77
Falke, R., 96
Fanous, S., 41
Fedor-Freybergh, P., 98–99
Fenu, S., 29
Fibiger, H. C., 76–77, 117
Fiorillo, C. D., 76
Fisher, C., 54
Fisher, S., 73
Fiss, H., xii, 6–9, 31, 39–40, 48, 54, 63, 65–66, 78–79, 81, 101
Fitzgerald, J., 27
Fitzgerald, P. B., 94–95
Flowers, L. K., xii, 3, 6, 8–10, 14, 18, 20, 43, 47, 49–50, 64, 66
Foraita, R., 7, 13, 18, 32, 61
Fosshage, J. L., 78
Foster, K. L., 28
Foulkes, D., 71
Fowler, J. S., 27–29, 100
Frackowiak, R. S., 27
Franck, G., 71, 77, 94

Franey, C., xi–xii, 3, 6–7, 9, 11–13, 18, 31, 39–40, 42, 48, 55, 61, 63–64, 101
Franklin, T. R., 9, 26
Freud, S., xii–xv, 5, 8, 10, 54, 57, 78, 81–91, 96–97, 107
Friston, K. J., 27, 77
Frost, J. J., 100
Fujiwara, S., 6

Gaillard, J. M., 96
Galli, A., xiv, 10, 13, 36
Garavan, H., 29
Garcia, M., 28
Garma, L., 94–95
Gasbarrini, G., 37
Geertzen, J. H., 75
Gerevich, J., 64
Gessa, G. L., 37
Gigli, G. L., 29
Gil, R., 26
Gillispie, C., 7, 16, 50, 53
Gjedde, E. D. A., 100
Glod, C. A., 98
Gold, M. S., 26
Goldstein, R. Z., 27, 29, 100
Golmard, J. L., 94–95
Gordon, E., 71, 100
Gorelick, D. A., 100
Gorman, L. L., 98
Grace, A. A., 100
Grant, G., 27
Greenberg, J., 83
Greenberg, R. P., 73
Grey, C., 28
Grünbaum, A., 89–90
Guénole, F., 89–90
guilt, 14–15, 18–23, 40, 49–51, 54, 59, 65–66, 86, 104
Gujar, N., 79
Gupta, D. K., 75
Gürpinar, D., 10

Hajek, P., xi–xii, 6, 8–9, 11–12, 14, 16, 18, 34, 39, 42–43, 50, 54–55, 62–63, 101

Hakun, J., 26
Hall, C. S., 5–6
hallucination, 53
    fulfilment, 65, 80, 82–83, 105
    satisfaction, 53, 83
Happe, S., 7, 13, 18, 32, 61
Harper, D., 26
Hartmann, E., 54, 78–79, 96
Harvey, S. C., 28
Hayes, Z., 100
Heinze, M., 7, 13, 18, 32, 61
Heishman, S. J., 41
Heninger, G., 26
Henke, P. G., 100
Herling, S., 77
Hernandez, J. M., 6
Herr, S. R., xii, 3, 6–7, 12–14, 55
Herscovitch, P., 71, 77, 94
Higgins, H., 7, 47, 64
Hines, M. E., 98
Hirota, Y., 71, 100
Hobson, J. A., xiii, 71, 77, 90, 97
Hochstenbach, J., 75
Hoffman, E., 57
Hoffmann, H. C., 7
Hollister, L. E., 5
Hope, B. T., 41
Hu, P., 79
Huber, R., 31, 98
Humphreys, C. T., 29
Hunter, R. W., 78
Hutcheson, D. M., 25

Ikemoto, S., 29–30
Imperato, A., 27, 29
Insel, T. R., 76
Italian Society of Sleep Research (SIRS), xiv
Ivanets, N. N., 6

Jakobson, A. J., 94–95
Janiri, L., 37
Jasinski, D. R., 5, 100
Jasova, D., 98–99
Jayne, M., 29, 100
Jens, W., 26

Jerry, P. A., 6, 12, 39–40, 42, 47
Johnson, B., xii, 3, 6, 8, 10, 14, 16, 26, 39, 48, 57, 81–82, 97
Johnson, R. A., 3, 6–7, 50, 54–55, 57
Jolesz, F. A., 79
Jones, C. M., 28
Jones, D. S., 39
Jorgensen, E. D., 7, 47
June, H. L., 28

Kampman, K., 26
Kaplan, L., 96
Kaplan-Solms, K., 93
Kassel, J. D., 26
Kaufman, E., 5–6
Kay, D. C., 5
Keeley, J. D., 3, 7–8, 10, 47
Kelley, A. E., 76
Kenny, E. T., 29
Kibira, C., 6, 48, 50, 53, 62–63
Kim, Y. K., 100
Kimes, A. S., 100
Klawans, H. L., 96
Kleber, H. D., 29
Klein, G. S., 54
Kleitman, N., 5
Kline, P., 73
Kolivakis, T., 29
Koob, G. F., 25, 27–30, 32, 41, 76, 101
Kramer, M., 6, 40, 72, 78
Krasnicki, S., 26
Krotick, S., 39
Krystal, J. H., 26
Kukleta, M., 98
Kumar, A., 100
Kupfer, D., 71, 77, 94
Kuwabara, H., 100

Lagrutta, A., xiv, 10, 13, 36
Lane, I., 78
Langleben, D., 26
Lansky, L., 72
Laplanche, J., 83
Larimer, M. E., 48
LeDoux, J., 31
Lee, G. P., 98

Le Moal, M., 25, 32, 41, 76, 101
Levin, R., 78
Lewis, S. A., 5
Leyton, M., 29
Li, Y., 26
Lieberman, M. D., 76
Limbic System Check List (LSCL-33), 98–99
Ling, W., 6, 47, 64
Links, J., 100
Listerud, J., 26
Liu, Y., 76
Logan, J., 29, 100
Lohoff, F. W., 26
London, E. D., 27
Looney, M., 5–7, 13, 17, 32, 41, 65
Lucchetti, R., 96
Luxen, A., 71, 77, 94

Maas, J. W., 5
Maddahian, E., 6, 47
Makaric, E., xii, 6, 40, 62, 85
Maloney, T., 29, 100
Manna, V., 26
Maquet, P., 71, 77, 94
Marcaggi, G., 89–90
Maremmani, I., 26, 32, 41
Maris, M. A., 100
Marlatt, G. A., 48
Marques, K., 26
Marrone, G. F., 41
Marshall, S., 6, 18, 48
Mason, D., 28
Massetani, R., 96
Matsumoto, K., 6
Mazzoni, P., 29
McCane, S., 28
McCann, M. J., 6, 47, 64
McCarley, R. W., 71, 77
McElgin, W., 27
McEwing, W., 6, 48
McKay, P. F., 28
Meggyes, K., 64
Meil, W. M., 29
Melis, M. R., 76
Merino-Andreu, M., 94–95

mesolimbic–mesocortical
   dopaminergic circuit, xii, 10,
   27–28, 30–31, 76, 79, 82, 94,
   96–99
Meyers, A., 6, 63
mid-brain ventral tegmental area
   (VTA), 27–28, 31
Miller, J. M., 29
Miller, N. S., 26
Mintun, M., 71, 77, 94
Miscia, A., xiv, 10, 13, 36
Mitchell, S. A., 83
Mitchison, G., xiii, 77
Moneme, A., 96
Money, J., 75
Monti, P. M., 26
Montoya, I. D., xii, 3, 6–7, 12–14, 55
Mooney, A. J., 6, 10, 12, 40, 43, 55,
   63
Moore, R. A., 5–6, 71, 77, 94
Morales, M., 41
Morris, J., 27
Morrison, A. P., 39
Morrison, R. A., 6, 53, 64
Moscovitz, C., 96
Moses, H., 96
Mozley, P. D., 27
Mulder, T. H., 75
Muzio, J. N., 5

Nader, K., 77
Naqvi, N. H., 29
Nausieda, P., 96
Nelson, R., 100
Nestler, E. J., 27–29
Newton, P., 75
Niaura, R. S., 26
Nielsen, T. A., 78
Nigro, G., 29
Nofzinger, E., 71, 77, 94
nucleus accumbens (NAc), 27–29, 31,
   76, 98
Nutt, D. J., 27

Obert, J. L., 6, 47, 64
O'Brien, C. P., 26–27

Oldfield, M., 96
Oliveira, M., 7, 11, 30–31, 47–48, 50,
   53
Ornstein, P. H., 6, 40, 72
Oswald, I., 5
Oswald, J., 5
Oudiette, D., 94–95

Pace-Schott, E. F., 77, 90
Pacini, M., 26
Palmer, R. S., 48
Panksepp, J., 29–31, 82, 94, 98
Paradiso, S., 29
Parker, J., 3, 6–7, 11, 64
Pavlick, M., 57
Paxton, D. A., 29
Pedraza, M., 26
Perantie, D. C., xi, 6, 8–9, 12–14, 19,
   32, 41, 43, 55, 63–64
Perogamvros, L., 79
Persico, A. M., xi–xii, 6, 10, 31, 39, 53,
   55, 62–63, 101
Peters, J. M., 71, 77, 94
Peters, K. A., 6, 12, 48, 53, 62, 64, 81
Peterson, N. D. J., 100
Petrakis, I. L., 26
Pfaus, J. G., 29, 76–77
Phillips, A. G., 29, 76–77, 117
Piani, A., 29
Piccini, P., 96
Piccoloto, L. B., 7, 11, 30–31, 47–48,
   50, 53
Pickens, C. L., 41
Pierce, C. M., 5
Piomelli, D., 28
Pivik, R. T., 5
Polcari, A., 98–99
Pontalis, J.-B., 83
Pontieri, F. E., 29
Popper, K., 89
prefrontal cortex, 27, 31, 79, 98
Preston, K. L., xii, 3, 6–7, 12–14, 41, 55
Pulvirenti, L., 27, 29

Raboch, J., 98
Ramsey, G. W., 73

Rao, V., 79
Rawson, R. A., 6, 47, 64
Reed, H., 6, 64
regulation, 30, 94
    function, xii, 8, 106
    imbalance, 82
    mood, 78
    process, 79
    up-, 30, 82, 97–101, 108
Reid, S. D., xi, 4, 6, 8–9, 12–14, 18, 20,
    42–43, 56, 62–64
Reivich, M., 27
Renshaw, P. F., 98–99
Revonsuo, A., 78
Richardson, E. D., 98
Riggle, T. A., 98
Robbins, T. W., 25
Roberts, R. J., 98
Robinson, T. E., 25–26, 29–30, 82, 94,
    97, 100
Robledo, P., 28
Roffwarg, H. P., 5
Rohde, C., 100
Rohsenow, D. J., 26
Romo, R., 77
Rose, J. E., 29
Rosenberg, H., 57
Ross, L., 71, 100
Rousset, O., 100
Rudrauf, D., 29
Ruggiero, S., 26
Russ, D., 96
Ryan, J., 75

Sacks, O., 96
Sahu, S. C., 75
Saletin, J. M., 79
Salwen, R., 7, 47
Sardi, D., xiv, 3, 7–8, 10–13, 34–36,
    98–101
Schredl, M., 6, 53, 64
Schretlen, D. J., 100
Schultz, W., 76–77
Schuster, C. R., 77
Schwartz, S., 79, 94–95
Sciortino, N., 26

Scott, E. M., 3, 5–6, 18
See, R. E., 29
Selbie, S., 71, 77, 94
self, 105
    -administration, 14, 27–28, 32
    -aversive, 54, 58, 62
    -protection, 55
    -reported, 98
    -stimulation, 27
Seligman, M., xiii, 77
Sell, L. A., 27
Sera, M., 6
sexual
    content, 88
    desire, 30–31
    dream, 36
    drive, 76
    impulse, 88
    motive, 88
    need, 84
    orgasm, 13, 75
    wishes, 89
Seyoum, R., 28
Shaham, Y., 41
Shalev, U., 41
Sharpe, D., 5–6, 21, 48
Shevrin, H., xii, 8, 10, 82
Shiffman, S., 26
Shingai, N., 6
Shukla, G. D., 75
Simeon, D. T., xi, 4, 6, 8–9, 12–14, 18,
    20, 42–43, 56, 62–64
Skoff, B., 96
Skolnick, P., 28
Smaldino, A., 6
Smith, K. S., 28
Smith, M. R., 71, 100
Solms, M., xii, 71, 77, 89–90, 93,
    95–101
Sperandio, R., xiv, 3, 7–8, 10–13,
    34–35, 98–101
Steiner, S. S., 5
Steinig, J., 7, 13, 18, 32, 61
Stewart, C., 6, 39
Stickgold, R., 77, 90
Stinus, L., 32, 41, 101

subject(s), 5, 17, 21–22, 34, 36–37,
    55, 74–75, 85, 93, 98,
    100–101
  addicted, 34, 99, 101
  deprived, 40, 53–54, 74
  unaware, 27
subjective(ly), 29, 77
  emotionality, 79
substance abuse see:
    drug abuse
Suh, J., 26
Surrey, J., 98
Světlák, M., 98
Swanson, J. M., 27–28
Swett, C., 98
Szupszynski, K., 7, 11, 30–31, 47–48,
    50, 53

Tafti, M., 94–95
Takao, H., 6
Tanda, G., 29
Tart, C. T., 5
Teicher, M. H., 98–99
Telang, F., 29, 100
Theberge, F., 41
theory see also: dream(s)
  aversive conditioning, 54
  emotional
    adaptive, 78
    dissipation, 7
  Freudian, 87, 107
  of psychic apparatus, 83
  psychoanalytic, xii, 90
    neuro-, xii
  reverse learning, 77
Tindell, A. J., 28
Tobler, P. N., 76
Tokçoğlu, L., 10
Tomasi, D., 29, 100
Tracy, J. I., 18
Tranguch, A. J., 29
Trevisan, L., 26
Tripathi, R. P., 75
Tuci, B., xiii
Tucker, M. A., 71, 100
Turnbull, O., 93, 95, 98

Uguccioni, G., 94–95
unconscious(ness), 82, 87, 104–105
    see also: conscious(ness)
  ally, 87–88
  aspects, 27, 49
  craving, 30, 48, 81
  desire, 48
  drive, 82
  level, 35, 52
  perception, 27
  process, 48
  rejection, 86–87

Vaidya, J. G., 29
Valli, K., 90
Van der Helm, E., 79
van der Kooy, D., 77
Van Gorp, W. G., 29
Varga, M., 71, 77, 94
Varney, N. R., 98
Vijayaraghavan, L., 29
Vinnikova, M. A., 6
Violani, C., xiii
Vogel, G. W., 90
Volkow, N. D., 27–30, 100
Vorel, S. R., 29

Walker, M. P., 79
Wamsley, E. J., 71, 100
Wang, G. J., 27–29, 100
Wang, Z., 26
Washton, A. M., 3, 6, 18, 55
Waterhouse, K., 5–6
Webb, E., 26
Weber, S., 96
Weinberg, A. N., 6
Weiner, W., 96
Weinstein, A., 27
Wenkstern, D., 77
Wesenten, N. J., 71, 77, 94
Whitman, R. M., 5–6, 40, 72
Wise, R. A., 28, 76, 100
Wiseman, M., 71, 77, 94
withdrawal, 4, 41, 63
  cigarette, 53
  of cathexis, 87

symptoms, 26, 34–35, 41, 43, 56
syndrome, 4, 43
Woicik, P. A., 29, 100
Wolf, M. E., 30
Wong, C., 29, 100
Wong, D. F., 100
Wood, P., 74
Woods, J. E., 28
Wright, J., 30–31
Wurmser, L., 6

Yao, J., 79
Yap, J., 41
Yee, T., xi, 6, 8–9, 12–14, 19, 32, 41, 43,
    55, 63–64
Yellen, A., xiii, 77

Yeming, M., 29, 100
Yin, W., 28
Yonezawa, H., 6
Yoo, S. S., 79
Young, A. M., 77
Yu, C. K.-C., 94–95, 101
Yu, Y. J., 76

Zarcone, V., 5
Zhou, Y., 100
Ziegler, P. P., 9, 27, 32
Zolesi, O., 32, 41
Zukin, S., 100
Zweben, J. E., xii, 3, 6, 8–10,
    14, 18, 20, 43, 47, 49–50, 64,
    66